—African-American Biographies—

LORRAINE HANSBERRY

Playwright and Voice of Justice

Series Consultant:
Dr. Russell L. Adams, Chairman
Department of Afro-American Studies, Howard University

Catherine Scheader

Enslow Publishers, Inc.

40 Industrial Road	PO Box 38
Box 398	Aldershot
Berkeley Heights, NJ 07922	Hants GU12 6BP
USA	UK

http://www.enslow.com

Library of Congress Cataloging-in-Publication Data

Scheader, Catherine.
    Lorraine Hansberry: playwright and voice of justice / Catherine Scheader.
        p. cm. — (African-American biographies)
    Includes bibliographical references and index.
    Summary: A biography of the playwright who was the first black
    person and the youngest American to receive the New York Drama
    Critics Circle award for the best play of the year.
    ISBN 0-89490-945-2
    1. Hansberry, Lorraine, 1930–1965—Juvenile literature. 2. Women dramatists,
American—20th century—Biography—Juvenile literature.
3. Afro-American dramatists—Biography—Juvenile literature. 4. Afro-Americans in
literature—Juvenile literature. [1. Hansberry, Lorraine, 1930–1965. 2. Dramatists,
American. 3. Afro-Americans—Biography. 4. Women—Biography.] I. Title. II. Series.
PS3515.A515Z87 1998
812'.54—dc21
[B]
97-35798
                                                                    CIP
                                                                    AC
Printed in the United States of America

10 9 8 7 6 5 4

Excerpts from the following works are gratefully acknowledged:

From COLLECTED POEMS by Langston Hughes Copyright © 1994 by the Estate
of Langston Hughes. Reprinted by permission of Alfred A. Knopf Inc.

Excerpt from "Sweet Lorraine" by James Baldwin. Originally published in
Esquire. Collected in THE PRICE OF THE TICKET © 1985 by James Baldwin.
Reprinted by arrangement with the James Baldwin Estate.

Reprinted with the permission of Simon & Schuster from TO BE YOUNG, GIFT-
ED AND BLACK: LORRAINE HANSBERRY IN HER OWN WORDS adapted by
Robert Nemiroff. Copyright © 1969 by Robert Nemiroff and Robert Nemiroff as
Executor of the Estate of Lorraine Hansberry.

Illustration Credits:
Courtesy, Estate of Robert Nemiroff, pp. 6, 19, 31, 42, 51, 71, 78, 83, 86, 102, 107,
110, 112; Photographs and Prints Division, Schomburg Center for Research in
Black Culture, The New York Public Library, Astor, Lenox and Tilden
Foundations, pp. 10, 29, 56, 65, 74, 93; Gin Briggs, photographer, p. 47; Gail A.
Hansberry, p. 27.

Cover Illustration: Courtesy, Estate of Robert Nemiroff

CONTENTS

To Ed with love and gratitude

Acknowledgments

I am grateful to members of Lorraine Hansberry's family for their warm recollections: her sister, Mamie Hansberry Mitchell, and her cousins Shauneille Perry and Gail Hansberry. My debt to the late Robert Nemiroff, Ms. Hansberry's former husband, who faithfully preserved and celebrated her work, is immense. Generous with interview time, he patiently answered questions and served as my guide to the world of theater. Jewell Gresham Nemiroff, his widow and current keeper of the flame, was encouraging, supportive, and the source of many photos. Thanks are also due to Ms. Hansberry's colleagues, producer Philip Rose, and director Lloyd Richards, for answers to my inquiries. I wish to thank staff members of the New York Public Library, particularly James Huffman of the Schomburg Center, for able assistance with photo research. My editor, Nina Rosenstein, has been cheerful and tireless throughout the project, and I thank her for professional support. Finally, I want to acknowledge friends in the Bridgewater Writers for Children group and my family, who read and responded to the manuscript.

Lorraine Hansberry

1

OPENING NIGHT

On March 11, 1959, applause thundered through the Ethel Barrymore Theatre in New York. The opening night audience was roaring its approval of Lorraine Hansberry's new play, *A Raisin in the Sun*. Wide-eyed and unbelieving, Hansberry watched cast members bow again and again to the cheering crowd. Then actor Sidney Poitier signaled for quiet and called her name. Hansberry gave her husband's hand a last squeeze and stepped past him as shouts of "Author, author!" surrounded her. She hurried down the aisle, a rope of pearls swinging in front of her slim black dress.

Poitier reached down to help as strong arms lifted

her on either side, and Hansberry felt herself swept up onto the stage. The cheering began again, thundering from every level of the theater. Breathless, she waved and blew kisses. Almost directly below was her family, sitting front and center. She saw the proud look on Mama's face and her sister's wide smile. At that moment, Hansberry wanted more than anything else to hug them and ask what they thought of "little sister" now.[1]

Two months earlier, she had written to her mother from a Connecticut hotel on the night of the play's first tryout. "The actors are very good and the director is a very talented man," Hansberry wrote. "So if it is a poor show I won't be able to blame a soul but your youngest child."[2]

Before tonight, Hansberry knew, no one had ever seen so many African Americans in a Broadway theater. But then, this was the first serious Broadway drama about an African-American family.

In the letter to her mother, Hansberry had written,

> Mama, it is a play that tells the truth about people. . . .
> I think it will help a lot of people to understand how we
> are just as complicated as they are—and just as mixed
> up—but above all, that we have among our miserable
> and downtrodden ranks—people who are the very
> essence of human dignity. That is what, after all the
> laughter and tears, the play is supposed to say. I hope it
> will make you very proud.[3]

When Hansberry began writing the play three years earlier, she never anticipated this night and this reaction. At that time, she was also working on a novel and an opera. But more and more, the play absorbed her completely. She worked on it for eight more months, between her twenty-sixth and twenty-seventh birthdays.

The characters Hansberry created became real enough to talk to—like people she had grown up with on the South Side of Chicago. She knew their thoughts and what they would say. She could picture their well-worn apartment, similar to apartments she had walked through in her childhood.[4]

Almost from the beginning, Hansberry knew the Younger family's story had to be a play. She wanted her words spoken directly from the stage. For Hansberry, the play was a way of carrying on a conversation with the audience. The conversation she created was very selective, with sharply defined characters and conflict.[5]

Tonight, a New York audience looked into the stage set of a tiny South Side Chicago kitchen and saw a hardworking African-American woman with a dream. The audience heard her family's astonishment at learning that she was moving them to a clean, uncrowded neighborhood—an all-white neighbor-hood. The house was in a section of the city where this dark-skinned family was clearly unwelcome.

Stories of women's dreams were not new in the theater,

Lorraine Hansberry

Ruby Dee, Sidney Poitier (center), and Lonnie Elder, III, in *A Raisin in the Sun.*

nor were conflicts between parents and children. New in this play was a particular African-American family living on the South Side of Chicago.[6]

At the cast party later that night, Hansberry, her husband, Bob Nemiroff, their families, and everyone connected with producing the play gathered to celebrate. While they relived the earlier excitement and congratulated one another, the room crackled with tension. Although the audience had made its enthusiasm clear, some very important people were still to be heard from. They were the drama critics who wrote reviews of new plays in the New York City newspapers.

Good reviews would bring people to the theater box office to buy tickets. The more tickets sold, the longer the run of the play. Actors, the theater owner, and even the custodians could look forward to a steady income for months or even years. On the other hand, a poor review in a New York newspaper could shut down a play in the first few days or weeks.

Everyone at the party watched the clock that night, waiting for the early-morning newspapers. The suspense ended when copies of *The New York Times* and *The New York Herald-Tribune* arrived. Theater critics for both newspapers praised the play. The next day, other newspapers carried enthusiastic accounts of *A Raisin in the Sun*. Lorraine Hansberry's first play was a great success.

Hansberry was unprepared for the kind of attention that followed. An unknown playwright before opening night, she was suddenly the talk of the town. Everyone, it seemed, wanted to see her, hear her, and photograph her. Newspaper and magazine writers called her for interviews. Requests for radio and television appearances poured in.[7]

To people in the African-American community, the play was a special gift, a story of ordinary people who did extraordinary things. Hansberry had taken the African-American experience to a place it had never been before. *A Raisin in the Sun* was emblazoned on Broadway alongside the usual dramas about white people. African-American organizations deluged her with requests to speak at meetings and dinners. Hansberry and Nemiroff accepted invitations to parties for months afterward.

Twenty to thirty pieces of mail arrived every day. For Hansberry, the words of appreciation were her reward for hours of struggle writing the play. She attempted to answer every letter.

When a writer from *The New Yorker* magazine called for an interview, Hansberry asked to meet him in a midtown restaurant to get away from the phone. "The telephone has become a strange little thing with a life of its own," she said.[8] Hansberry and Nemiroff changed their number and gave the new one to only a few people. But the phone kept on ringing.

In interviews, Hansberry explained that the Younger family in *A Raisin in the Sun* was not her own family. She was too close to write about them, she explained.[9] But the conversations with reporters about life on the South Side of Chicago prompted vivid memories of the time she had lived there, not so many years before.

2

ON THE SOUTH
SIDE OF CHICAGO

Lorraine Vivian Hansberry was born May 19, 1930, in Chicago, Illinois. She was the youngest of Nanie Perry Hansberry and Carl Augustus Hansberry's four children. Lorraine's mother, who had trained to be a teacher in her home state of Tennessee, came to Chicago as a young woman. Born in Glaston, Mississippi, Mr. Hansberry was a college graduate and a lawyer.

Growing up in the South, both Mr. and Mrs. Hansberry were familiar with legal discrimination against African Americans. In the North, they experienced other forms of racial discrimination. Northern schools and public facilities could not legally exclude blacks. But Northern whites found ways to keep the races separate. In the 1930s, local laws permitted distinct African-American and white neighborhoods in Chicago. Children attended neighborhood schools that were, in fact, segregated by race. Grown-ups did their shopping in local stores and attended neighborhood churches and movies.

As a result of the housing discrimination, African Americans of every social class lived side by side on crowded South Side streets. Although the Hansberrys were financially well-off, they lived in a poor neighborhood. As the owner of a successful real estate agency, with a good income, Mr. Hansberry was able to provide luxuries his neighbors could not afford. The family owned a car and had a maid to help with the housework. Like many small-business owners, Mr. Hansberry was a member of the Republican Party. Proud to be an American, he believed strongly in his country's ideals.[1]

Lorraine learned about the differences between her family and their neighbors when she was still in kindergarten. For days before that Christmas, she had stared at a large and interesting-looking package under the tree. Knowing it was her present, she tried to guess its contents. On Christmas morning, she tore at the wrappings while aunts and uncles smiled and nudged one another.

As her mother shook out the small, white fur coat,

Lorraine could only stare. The grown-ups broke into "oohs" and "ahs," and no one seemed to notice that Lorraine was close to tears. Heart sinking, she felt her arms being pushed into silky sleeves and a matching cap being pulled over her bouncy curls. Her mother swung a muff, hanging from a cord, round her neck. The fur muff would keep her hands warm. Lorraine could not believe that she was expected to wear this coat to kindergarten!

On the street where the Hansberrys lived, children covered holes in the soles of their shoes with scraps of cardboard, even in the middle of winter. These grown-ups should know the trouble this coat would cause! How could anyone call it a Christmas present?[2]

On the first day back to school after Christmas vacation, Lorraine raced home. Sobbing and pelted with mud balls, she tried to outrun a horde of shouting kids. They scattered only when she flung herself at the front door.

Her mother dried the tears and talked to her about jealousy. Lorraine listened and tried to understand why these older, tougher children were jealous of her. After that day, she began to notice other differences between those children and her own sister, brothers, and cousins.

The housing laws in Chicago that set aside neighborhoods for whites only were called "restrictive covenants." Those laws had been enforced for more than a decade before Lorraine was born. They prevented African Americans from buying or renting houses and apartments in many areas of the city.

Mr. Hansberry saw apartments in white neighborhoods sit empty while African-American families on the South Side doubled up, waiting to occupy an apartment. He and other real estate agents were determined to challenge the restrictive covenants. They believed all citizens, regardless of color, should be able to live in homes they could afford.

When Lorraine was young, conversations in the Hansberry kitchen about the housing problem continued late into the night. Relatives and friends gathered and planned strategies to overturn the unfair laws. Lorraine overheard bits of talk that she did not understand.

Then one day in 1938, when Lorraine was eight years old, her father gathered the family together. He announced a plan to challenge the unfair laws. Mr. Hansberry had bought a house on an all-white block. Soon after, the family moved into the first-floor apartment of the house.

Mr. Hansberry knew the city would order him to give up the apartment. When the eviction order came, he was ready to act. He brought a lawsuit against the city of Chicago in the state court of Illinois. The lawsuit sought to make restrictive covenants illegal.

Lorraine Vivian Hansberry, the youngest of four children, grew up on the South Side of Chicago.

Preparing and arguing the case kept Mr. Hansberry away from home for weeks at a time. He stayed in Springfield, the state capital, where the case was heard. At home, Lorraine's mother looked after the family.[3]

Lorraine transferred to the Sexton School, where all but a few children were white. There she encountered racial prejudice for the first time. White children at school and in the neighborhood refused to play with her. They said cruel things, telling her to go back where she belonged. When they taunted her about her skin color, Lorraine swallowed hard and looked them in the eye, as her parents had taught her. It was scary, but she knew she was as smart as they were. And she knew they were wrong to taunt her.

Lorraine's few good friends still lived in her old neighborhood, so she had nothing to do but hang around the front porch after school . Her sister, Mamie, eight years older, was the only bright spot. Mamie's job was to look after Lorraine. Mamie missed her own friends too, but she stuck close to her little sister. More than Lorraine, she knew how important the lawsuit was. And she knew that living in this white neighborhood could be dangerous. No one wanted the Hansberrys there.

One afternoon, Lorraine was swinging her feet on the porch rail when Mamie suddenly pushed her into the house. Lorraine had time for only a quick backward glance. Across the street, a small but noisy crowd was gathering. Mamie slammed the door shut.

Inside, Mrs. Hansberry told them to keep away from the windows but not to worry. She said the white people were curious about their new dark-skinned neighbors. She was expecting Lorraine's teenaged brothers to return home soon. Mrs. Hansberry sounded calm when she reminded the girls that the maid and a friend of their father's were there in the house with them. Lorraine knew the friend was really a bodyguard, hired for protection while her father was away. Still, she could feel the grown-ups' worry as the crowd grew larger and noisier.[4]

By the time her brothers, Carl and Perry, came home, shouts from outside filled the front room. Lorraine could not resist peeking out. At that moment, the front window exploded in a shower of glass and something rocketed into the room. Narrowly missing her, the large object thudded against a wall and crashed to the floor. Screaming, Lorraine let Carl and Perry rush her into a back room.

Lorraine cried herself to sleep. When she woke, the street was quiet. Cardboard replaced the broken glass in the window. A jagged chunk of concrete, the size of a football, sat on a kitchen chair. Lorraine shivered when she saw the object that had almost hit her. She learned that the bodyguard, with his gun drawn, had scared away the crowd.

Lorraine was sure her parents would move back to the old neighborhood. But on a short break from his court case, Mr. Hansberry announced they were staying. The city could not evict them until the case was settled. After he returned to the state capital, Lorraine's mother patrolled the house every night with a loaded gun. She was ready to protect her family.[5] Friends stopped in more often, and Lorraine saw African-American cab drivers cruise slowly past the house. She knew that people were looking after them.[6]

The Hansberrys lived in the house for almost a year. Not until Mr. Hansberry lost his case against the state of Illinois did he obey the court order to leave. But the loss did not end his resistance. The state court's decision was only one battle in the war against Chicago's restrictive covenants. Believing in the justice of his cause, Carl Augustus Hansberry fought on.

3

OTHER VOICES

ack on the South Side, the family no longer had neighbors to fear. Lorraine slipped into old, familiar routines. Betsy Ross Elementary School, overcrowded and segregated, operated on half-day sessions. Each year, Lorraine fell further behind in mathematics. Reading was her best subject, and books filled her afternoons at home. Except on the coldest days, girls jumped rope in the street outside her house. Lorraine watched their flying feet, knowing she could never skip double Dutch that fast.[1]

Once again, she was "little sister." While Mamie, Carl, and Perry zipped in and out between dates and sporting events, she buried herself in books. Only when cousin Shauneille Perry stayed over did she have someone her age to talk to.

One summer, Lorraine's mother took the two girls to Columbia, Tennessee, where she had grown up. On the long, dusty ride, Nanie Perry Hansberry pointed out the Kentucky hills where her own father had hidden after he escaped from slavery. The girls met their Grandmother Perry for the first time that summer. Lorraine was startled that the woman whom all the grown-ups had always called "a great beauty" was very old and wrinkled. Born in slavery, she told stories of her childhood as a slave. None of them sounded a bit like *Gone With the Wind,* a movie about the South that Lorraine had seen.[2]

In Columbia, aunts and uncles made a fuss over "Nanie and Graham's girls." Uncle George, who had stayed in Tennessee to farm when his sister and brothers went north, treated the city girls to their first ride on a horse. Clinging to a burlap bag thrown over the horse's back, Lorraine and Shauneille struggled to hold on. Everyone laughed when Shauneille fell off.[3]

Back in Chicago on steamy nights, the family found shelter in the park from their sizzling apartment. Those were the best times because the grown-ups talked about their childhood memories. Lying on a blanket, Lorraine looked up at the sky and watched while her father pointed to the stars. He told her how far away they were, and the distances were hard for her to imagine.

Through open windows in the summer, Lorraine heard other voices. All around her, people struggled with the problems of life, made more intense by poverty and lack of opportunity. She heard mothers of sick children with no money for doctors or medicine. Discouraged men kept on looking for work. Families in tiny apartments quarreled. But laughter and music also rang from the windows. And in the neighborhood voices, Lorraine heard love and hope.

The grown-ups' endless conversations continued around the Hansberrys' kitchen table. Mr. Hansberry was home more often, preparing his lawsuit for the United States Supreme Court. He and Mrs. Hansberry also fought other forms of discrimination. Refused service at a Chicago restaurant one day because of their color, the Hansberrys stood up for their rights. While Mr. Hansberry went for the police, his wife waited in the restaurant doorway.[4]

Mamie graduated from high school and enrolled at Howard University in Washington, D.C. Founded by African Americans, the school had a faculty that was committed to educating African Americans to become leaders. Unlike the segregated Chicago schools, Howard enjoyed an excellent reputation. Mamie hoped to concentrate on studying and making friends without the distractions of racial issues.[5] Howard

University was also part of a family tradition. Mr. Hansberry's brother, William Leo, was a professor of African history at Howard. At holiday celebrations with the Chicago Hansberrys, Uncle Leo often brought along students who were visiting from Africa.

Listening to the African students, Lorraine learned about the great continent of her ancestors. And the students learned from discussions at the Hansberry dinner table. There they heard about life in the United States and, in particular, a large northern city.

Mr. Hansberry's brother-in-law, Horace Fitchett, was also a Howard University professor. A sociologist, Uncle Horace studied how people of different races and back-grounds behaved and related to one another. Cousin Shauneille's father, Graham Perry, was a lawyer and an assistant attorney general for the state of Illinois. Uncle Graham talked about the untapped political power of African Americans. Lorraine's father brought a busi-nessman's point of view to the discussions.

Famous African Americans made the Hansberry home a stopping place when they were in Chicago. They added their ideas to conversations around the table. One frequent guest, W. E. B. Du Bois, was the first African American to earn a Ph.D. from Harvard University. The author of scholarly books and articles, Du Bois advocated integration of white and black soci-ety. He agreed with Mr. Hansberry that integrated neighborhoods were the key to equality of the races.

When Uncle William Leo Hansberry, professor of African history at Howard University, came to visit, he often brought along some of his students from Africa.

Singer and actor Paul Robeson was a close family friend. Outspoken about unjust laws, Robeson was thought by many to be un-American. Threats on his life had made him cautious about traveling, and he never announced his visits in advance.[6]

With family or famous guests, talk looped between history and current events, between Africa and the United States. The dinner table, with its many visiting experts, provided a richer educational experience than any classroom. During those family gatherings, Lorraine absorbed language, history, racial pride, and politics.

Mr. and Mrs. Hansberry did not demand *A*'s from their children. They supervised homework and made sure the children were learning to think, read, and write. Mr. Hansberry encouraged them to express opinions, but required facts for backup.

The year 1940 was a time of mixed blessings for the Hansberrys. On the downside, Mr. Hansberry lost his bid for Congress on the Republican ticket. But later that year, he finally won his lawsuit against the city of Chicago.

The United States Supreme Court ruled that the laws permitting restrictive covenants to separate African-American and white neighborhoods violated the Constitution of the United States. By law, according to the decision, no one could use skin color to exclude people from homes or apartments. The

Paul Robeson with accompanist Lawrence Brown in 1938. Robeson, the famous singer, actor, and political activist, was a close family friend of the Hansberrys.

landmark case, *Hansberry* v. *Lee*, is still studied in law schools.

Despite the decision, change was slow, and resistance from the white community continued. In the next few years, World War II brought many more African Americans from the South to Chicago for jobs in defense factories and stockyards. Even with added pressure from the newcomers, South Side boundaries were slow to expand.

In 1944, young Carl was in the armed services. Perry, refusing to serve in a segregated army, contested his draft notice and became a conscientious objector.[7] The armed services were not desegregated until three years later, after the war ended.

Mr. Hansberry's lifelong hope for better race relations was beginning to fade. He bought a house in Mexico, planning for retirement. But on vacation there in 1945, he died suddenly. His death was a terrible loss, but he had provided for his family. The older children operated the real estate agency and continued their parents' fight against housing discrimination.

Lorraine graduated from Betsy Ross Elementary School and went to Englewood High School, which was another segregated building. She loved to draw and thought about a career in art. Words also stirred her imagination.

Unlike her sister and brothers, Lorraine hardly ever went to sporting events. When she wanted to write

The Book of

Lorraine Hansberry

A Review of a Year,
January, 1947, to January, 1948.
ENGLEWOOD HIGH SCHOOL
CHICAGO, ILLINOIS

LORRAINE VIVIAN HANSBERRY
President, Forum
Gym secretary
To be a journalist

In her Englewood High School yearbook, Hansberry expressed
her interest in journalism.

an essay on football for a contest, she first interviewed Mamie and friends for information on the subject. Her essay won second prize.

In high school, Lorraine and Shauneille went to dances that the grown-ups arranged at social clubs. Parents always drove them and brought them home. Unlike Mamie, Lorraine was not particularly interested in clothes. Once, when her mother gave her money to buy a suit, Lorraine asked Mamie to choose one for her. While Mamie shopped, Lorraine slipped off to the library.[8]

Reading Shakespeare was at first a puzzle. But soon his humor and celebration of ordinary people drew her in. An English teacher who recognized Lorraine's ability urged her to work harder.

Although she was still torn between studying art or writing, Lorraine's desire to be a journalist appeared under her picture in the high school yearbook. High school staff members were no help with college planning. In fact, Lorraine was discouraged from applying to college at all. Only after Mrs. Hansberry insisted were her college applications signed and submitted by school officials.[9]

One thing was clear to Lorraine. College had to be better than Englewood High School!

4

THE FIRST
MELODY

orraine Hansberry knew she was expected to follow the family tradition and attend Howard University. But the University of Wisconsin, with its strong journalism program, attracted her. With her sister Mamie's help, she persuaded Mrs. Hansberry to let her apply to Wisconsin.[1]

With Mamie and their brother Perry, Hansberry drove to the Madison campus to start the spring semester in 1948. Although she had registered early enough for a dormitory room, no campus housing was available when she arrived. Instead, she moved into Langdon Manor, a small off-campus residence.

Langdon Manor housed a number of foreign students, but Hansberry was its first African American. She moved in and integrated the house.[2]

Almost from the beginning, the routine of college, with science labs and the need to take careful notes in class, overwhelmed Hansberry. Her high school preparation had been scanty, and she struggled with college math and science. She found it hard to see the purpose of some required courses. Like most large universities in the 1940s, Wisconsin required freshmen to take introductory courses in several subject areas. The courses were designed to provide a broad educational background for students. Hansberry found one required course, physical geography, particularly troublesome. Although higher marks in literature, history, and philosophy helped balance out low grades in required courses, she barely maintained a passing average.[3]

After looking forward to being on her own for so long, Hansberry tried to concentrate on the bright spots of college life. Winter snow that wrapped the campus in blue-white beauty lifted her spirits. Best of all, she made new friends. University students came from all over the United States and from other countries, including states in Africa. Lorraine's interest in that faraway continent, first stirred by Uncle Leo and his students, grew stronger.[4]

Campus political clubs also attracted her. She

joined the Young Progressive League and later became its president.[5] In 1948, when Henry Wallace ran for president of the United States as a third-party candidate, Hansberry worked on his campaign. Wallace hoped to draw traditional Democratic and Republican voters to his Progressive Party. The party's platform, which sought more power for working-class people, appealed to Hansberry.

Still, she studied and tried to pass her required courses. One night, cramming for an exam that she had little hope of passing, she decided to take a break. Closing her book, she wandered over to the campus theater. Onstage was a production of Sean O'Casey's *Juno and the Paycock*. Knowing nothing of the playwright or his work, she was stunned by his power. O'Casey had elevated ordinary lives into great literature. Waves of dialogue swept over her, bathing her in poetry. Watching the problems of one stage family unfold, Hansberry knew she was seeing the tragedy of all poor Irish people.[6]

The experience was unforgettable. Years later, she wrote, " . . . the melody was one that I had known for a very long while. . . . I did not think then of writing the melody as I knew it—in a different key; but I believe it entered my consciousness and stayed there."[7]

After two years at the University of Wisconsin, Hansberry felt she was wasting time. The last straw came with her grade in a course called Scenic Design.

She loved the course, which drew on her gift for art and design and her growing interest in the theater. Expecting an *A*, she was shocked by her failing grade. Convinced it was a mistake, she appealed to the instructor. He told her that he was sparing her from later disappointment. In his opinion, a black woman had no chance of succeeding in the theater.[8]

In January 1950, Hansberry telephoned her sister. "Do you think Mama would be upset if I didn't graduate?" she asked. Mamie suggested a trip home to talk things over.[9] That month, at the end of the semester, Hansberry left the University of Wisconsin. She stayed in Chicago, however, for only a few months.

That summer, Hansberry made plans to leave Chicago. Unlike Mamie, Carl, and Perry, who were busy managing the family real estate business, she had no ties to the city. By then she had her sights set on a journalism career. Eager to strike out on her own, Hansberry left for New York City.[10]

5

HARLEM STREET CORNERS

In New York, Hansberry was not quite alone. Like many other middle-class parents in the 1950s, her mother felt uneasy about a daughter living far from home in a large city. Mrs. Hansberry had contacted friends for Lorraine to turn to if help was needed.[1]

Hansberry moved into an apartment with three other women on the Lower East Side of Manhattan. The four rooms were a tight fit, but the young women were easy to get along with. Hansberry would have preferred living in Harlem, the famous African-American community uptown in the city. But apartments there were hard to find.

Still, she spent long hours in Harlem, working for *Freedom*, a new African-American newspaper founded by Paul Robeson. Since the end of World War II, in 1945, African-American opposition to racial discrimination had sharply increased. Yet few newspapers reported the protests or even general news about African Americans. Robeson published *Freedom* to highlight issues ignored in other publications.

Both the Harlem community and the rest of the city learned about the rising ferment from the pages of *Freedom*. An activist publication, *Freedom* was designed to energize African Americans to express their opinions and demand their rights as citizens. News stories highlighted African Americans on trial and contrasted the outcomes with similarly charged whites. Editorials mounted letter-writing campaigns to urge support for falsely accused African Americans.

Hired as a typist and receptionist, Hansberry handled subscriptions and some editing in the beginning. Soon her name appeared on book, film, and theater reviews. She quickly moved on to news articles and reporting of local, national, and global events.

In several columns, Hansberry protested radio and TV treatments of African Americans, noting the "shrill or lazy . . . dialect voices . . . of stereotypes . . . intended to give . . . a distorted and degraded image. . . ." She scorned, in particular, *The Beulah Show*, which featured "a giggling, contented domestic . . . who lives only to take care of her white employers and their children."

"The false and vicious impression . . . is no accident," she wrote. "The longer the concept of the half idiot, sub-human can be kept up, the easier to justify economic and every other kind of discrimination, so rampant in this country."[2]

Hansberry's job took her into the streets of Harlem. Attending meetings almost every night, she gathered local news and met the newsmakers. She joined the Harlem Youth Chorus and ushered at rallies in churches and in the Golden Gate Ballroom. Urging support for changes in the community, she made speeches on the corner of 125th Street and Seventh Avenue, outside Michael's Book Store. Like the South Side of Chicago, Harlem had to demand the public services that affluent city neighborhoods routinely received.

Hansberry took notes about her experiences. Surrounded by people of African heritage, she wrote:

> Sometimes in this country maybe just walking down a Southside street . . .
> Or maybe suddenly up in a Harlem window . . .
> Or maybe in a flash turning the page of one of those picture books from the South you will see it—
> *Beauty* . . . stark and full . . .
> No *part* of something this—but rather, Africa, simply Africa. These thighs and arms and flying wingèd cheekbones, these hallowed eyes—without negation or apology . . .
> *A classical people demand a classical art.*[3]

Random jottings in Hansberry's notebook expressed thoughts about her job. "The Negro people are a great people. They need a great newspaper," she scrawled across one page. And on another, "Read FREEDOM, Paul Robeson's newspaper."[4]

To a friend she wrote, *Freedom* "ought to be *the* journal of Negro liberation . . . in fact, it will be."[5]

Her hero was *Freedom*'s editor, Louis E. Burnham. Burnham was slightly built, but his appearance was forgotten in the power of his personality when he began to speak.

A large office window that overlooked the streets of Harlem kept Burnham close to his newspaper's readers. Hansberry spent hours in that office, listening and watching him move back and forth from the window. With a strong sense of history and language, he became her mentor. And both shared a love of those whom she thought of as "her" people.

One assignment took her to Ithaca in upstate New York. She went to report on what she called a "phony" youth meeting.[6] The conference had been called to respond to a Communist-sponsored, world youth rally held in East Berlin. The cold war, a period of hostility and distrust between the Soviet Union and the United States, was escalating. It was a time of widespread fear of Communist and Soviet agents. The fear led to suspicions about anything that sounded as if it might be Communist-inspired. Even those who advocated world peace or freedom from colonial rule were suspect. Hansberry's news article charged that the Ithaca conference was carefully controlled by the United States government. She noted the removal of the word *peace* from the agenda. And no discussion of freedom from colonial rule in Africa was planned. However, two Africans went beyond the official agenda. Hansberry applauded their demand for an end to European rule in their countries.

On another assignment, Hansberry reported in *Freedom* about a meeting of women in the District of Columbia. Adopting the name of Sojourner Truth, a famous evangelist and reformer, the group called itself the "Sojourners for Truth and Justice." The 132 women who attended came from all walks of life. They were the wives and mothers of victims of racial hatred and targets of injustice.[7]

Wrenching stories heard in the streets were shaking Hansberry's faith that African Americans would ever be treated as human beings. It was not only the unfair conditions that troubled her or the cruel remarks of people who ought to know better. Lynchings—murders by mobs that often hanged their victims—in Florida and Mississippi added an acute sense of horror to her apprehensions.

In Hansberry's meetings with Louis Burnham, the editor listened patiently, reminding her of the strength and dignity of African Americans. Hansberry caught

As a young woman, Lorraine Hansberry worked for *Freedom,* an African-American newspaper founded by Paul Robeson.

his sense of hope. Those who suffered so much would not only survive but prevail. In addition to sharing his faith in the future, Burnham encouraged her to set personal goals for herself.

As her writing assignments at *Freedom* increased, the journalism career Hansberry had dreamed of became a reality. In 1952, still just twenty-two years old, she was promoted to associate editor. In April 1952, she attended a peace conference in Montevideo, Uruguay. Hansberry was there as a substitute for Paul Robeson, whose passport had been canceled by the U.S. government because of his association with Communists. She described a warm welcome at the conference.

At the same time, stories she longed to write pounded in her imagination. Her thoughts kept returning to a novel begun and put aside two years earlier.[8]

The New School for Social Research in the Greenwich Village neighborhood of New York offered a college-level education. Unlike traditional schools such as the University of Wisconsin, the New School did not have course requirements. Adults were free to study subjects related to their interests. Hansberry enrolled in philosophy and writing courses.

In weeks crammed with work, school, and political activities, Hansberry still had time for fun. With friends, she haunted movie theaters that showed foreign films. In the late 1940s, Italian and French movies had invaded America. The stark, serious themes in some and manic comedy in others attracted a whole new group of bright young moviegoers.

Letters home teemed with Hansberry's new life and friends. More and more, she mentioned a man she had met on a picket line organized to protest New York University's segregated sports programs. Robert Barro Nemiroff, the son of Russian-Jewish immigrants who owned a downtown restaurant, attended New York University. He and Hansberry began dating in June 1952.

Like many of her new friends, Nemiroff was white. He shared Hansberry's fervor for ensuring the constitutional rights of all Americans.[9] She spent an increasing amount of time at the Nemiroff restaurant, getting to know his family and friends. On busy evenings, Hansberry sometimes showed restaurant patrons to their seats, and both she and Nemiroff occasionally waited on tables.

On her Christmas trip home to Chicago that year, Hansberry's mind whirled with a million thoughts. As the train rattled along, she tried to focus on what mattered most. While in Chicago, she wrote a long letter to Nemiroff that she immediately scrapped. In its place, she sent a brief note declaring her love for him and announcing an exciting idea for a play. The note ended with a ringing affirmation of her work. "I am a writer," she wrote, and, "I am going to write."[10]

On June 20, 1953, Hansberry and Nemiroff were married in Chicago at a ceremony attended by both families. Returning to New York, the couple moved into an apartment on Bleecker Street in the heart of Greenwich Village.

Nemiroff continued his graduate studies in literature at New York University while working at a part-time job. Hansberry left the *Freedom* staff and wrote only occasional pieces for the paper. She worked at undemanding jobs that paid expenses but left her mind free. True to the words of her Christmas letter, she began writing the stories that filled her thoughts. She started work on the first draft of a play.

In a letter to her husband while he was away on a trip, Hansberry wrote:

> I have re-read my play a couple of times to my disgust. . . . The truth is much of it *is* labored—much, however, reads well—and for the first time begins to approximate what I thought I wanted to say. Above all— I am beginning to think of the people *as people.* . . . I talk to them now and all that sort of thing.[11]

The play was not the only project that claimed Hansberry's attention. She also juggled a story for an opera and a novel.

Still, Hansberry continued working at a series of odd jobs. A department store, with African Americans making up less than one percent of its staff, turned down her application. But another store hired her as a typist. She also tagged coats for a furrier and served as a program leader with the New York Federation for the Handicapped.

An ad for production secretary on a Broadway play did not turn out as she'd hoped. Instead of providing a way into the world of the theater, her chief task was serving coffee. She immediately quit that job.

One position, directing programs at Camp Unity, an interracial adult camp, brought her to the countryside in Windfall, New York. For two weeks each year, she reveled in glorious sunrises and sunsets and gazed at scenic hills and trees around the lake. But although the camp experience usually inspired Hansberry, in the summer of 1954 she felt lost and discouraged there. Once again troubled by the state of human relations, she was probably also anxious about her writing.[12]

Hansberry and Nemiroff continued to support political causes but still had time for friends. With his longtime buddy Burt D'Lugoff, Nemiroff played guitar at neighborhood parties and college socials.

Another friend, Phil Rose, owned a small record company. In 1956 Rose agreed to record a group of four musicians (Vince Martin and the Tarriers, one of whom was actor Alan Arkin) whom Burt D'Lugoff

Lorraine Hansberry talks with campers at Camp Minisink in Port Jervis, New York, in 1960.

and his brother had discovered. All they needed was original music.

D'Lugoff approached Nemiroff. "Why don't we write a song?" he asked. "It shouldn't be that hard."[13] Playing with words and tunes, the two young men soon came up with, "Cindy, Oh Cindy." A lively tune and easy lyrics made it singable. Soon every disk jockey in New York was spinning the record. Stores sold out as fast as Phil Rose could deliver copies.

A huge hit in the summer of 1956, "Cindy, Oh Cindy" changed Hansberry's and Nemiroff's lives. Royalty income from record sales paid their expenses, and Nemiroff landed a well-paying position with Rose's recording company.

Hansberry quit her latest temporary job. The dream expressed in her December 1952 letter—"I am a writer"—had at last come true. From then on, she would fill her days with writing.

6

A SMALL WHITE DESK

At Christmastime in Chicago the year before "Cindy, Oh Cindy" hit the charts, Hansberry wrote in her journal, "My work. It is only here on paper that I dare say it like that: 'My work!'— So many truths seem to be rushing at me as the result of things felt and seen and lived through. Oh what I think I must tell this world! Oh the time that I crave— and the peace—and the *power*!"[1] A year later, without warning, the hit record gave her the gift of time she had craved. At last she could do the work she loved.

In the upstairs apartment on Bleecker Street, Hansberry worked at a typewriter on a small white desk in the bedroom. As usual, several writing projects were on the desk. But more and more, one play tugged at her. The story of a Chicago family with decisions to make, it was the play she was working on while her husband was away the year before. By now she knew her characters intimately.

The skills and conventions of playwriting are very different from those required for newspaper articles or even the fiction of short stories or novels. Hansberry had tried to write only one other play. She wrote this play, set in a steel mill, soon after coming to New York. While working on her new play, she was at the same time learning *how* to write a play.[2]

The story was clearer, but she still had dramatic problems to solve. The first act had come quickly, a rough draft written almost entirely in little more than a weekend. But that was almost a year ago, and now she found herself struggling. Sometimes she sat whole mornings at the typewriter, rearranging bits of dialogue and crumpling many sheets of paper.

Other times her ideas seemed stuck. She would pace the apartment from her desk in the bedroom, through an alcove lined with tall bookcases, into the living room. She stared into the fireplace or straightened prints of paintings hung on the green living room walls. But Michelangelo's and Pablo Picasso's images held no answers. Then she knew it was time to take her dog, Spice, a part-collie, for a walk.

Hansberry would clatter down the stairs of the

Hansberry wrote the first act of *A Raisin in the Sun* quickly. She knew her characters intimately.

two-story building and head for Christopher Street or for Tenth Street in the other direction. But she could not escape thoughts of her play. Back she would go, past the Chinese laundry and Spono's candy store, up the stairs. Sometimes the break worked, and she returned to her writing refreshed.[3]

Although Hansberry knew people in the theater and attended readings and workshops, she worked alone on her play, consulting no one. Unlike many other playwrights, she avoided workshops where a whole spectrum of theatrical people—directors, actors, and other writers—offered comments. Hansberry felt that she needed to shape her play almost to the finishing point before she could share it with anyone, even her husband.

During that year of intense writing, Hansberry met another writer who would later become a great friend. With work far along on her own play, she went one day to a workshop production of James Baldwin's *Giovanni's Room* at the Actors Studio. From her perch far up in the bleachers, she joined in the discussion at the end of the reading. Disputing the opinions of some important theater professionals, she praised the play. Afterward, she added more praise when she spoke to Baldwin himself.

Little by little through 1957 and 1958, Hansberry tightened her play, getting closer to the dramatic story she had imagined. Her characters were now very real to her. Not one of them was exactly like anyone she had known, but bits of many people emerged in their speech and motives. Voices that had surrounded her on the South Side of Chicago rang in the dialogue.

Hansberry reread the entire script one day and decided it was awful. She flung the pages at the ceiling and watched them fly around the room. Going for a broom to sweep the scattered sheets into the fireplace, she came back to see her husband down on his hands and knees, picking them up. She didn't see the script again for several days. Then one day, while she was moping around, Nemiroff put the pages in front of her. She went back to work and finished the play.[4]

In plotting her story, Hansberry wrote about choices—the limited choices of African Americans in the middle of the twentieth century. She wanted to show how people of courage could transcend their limitations. And she knew she had to involve her audience first with characters and only then with ideas. She had to tell a believable human story about people the audience would recognize and root for.

The family in her play was African American and poor. Unlike her own middle-class family, the Youngers resembled many of the neighbors she had known. She had spent time as a child in a number of kitchens like the Youngers'—in houses her father had rented to the poor, and on her own street.

Hansberry created a stern mother, a widow. This

mother loved her family so much that she would put them at risk to better their lives. Mrs. Younger was tired of living in a tiny, vermin-infested apartment, crowded in with a daughter, a son, his wife, and a young grandson.

Her family had other desires. Walter Lee, her son, wanted to break out of his chauffeuring job and go into business for himself. Beneatha, his sister, dreamed of going to medical school and becoming a doctor.

Mr. Younger, a postal employee, had died. As the play began, the check for his life insurance was about to arrive. Choices stemmed from what to do with the money. Mrs. Younger stunned the family by announcing her intention to buy a house for them in a middle-class, white neighborhood. Walter Lee's wife, Ruth, agreed with Mrs. Younger. Both women were passionate about escaping from their tiny apartment and crowded neighborhood. With part of the money, Mrs. Younger made a down payment on the house.

Implications of the move came straight from Hansberry's childhood, with whites trying to prevent blacks from moving into their neighborhood. But in the play, Hansberry concentrated the whites' resistance in a character, Karl Lindner, who offered money to the Youngers in return for not buying the home.

Walter Lee had his sights set on owning a liquor store. His recklessness almost cut off any choices. Instead of depositing the balance of the insurance check in the bank, he lost it in a bad business deal. Gone was the money for Beneatha's education, gone any cushion for the family's new life. For a brief moment, he was ready to accept the white man's offer. But his mother's call to pride turned the tide, and Walter Lee in the end chose to keep his human dignity. He announced to Lindner that the family had a right to live in their new house.

Hansberry had the most fun with the character of Beneatha, on whom she conferred some of her own traits. She knew that her sister and brothers would recognize their younger sister in the character. Beneatha's friend from Africa was based on students Uncle Leo had brought to the Hansberry home. He also resembled African students Hansberry had known at the University of Wisconsin.[5]

Working and reworking the script, Hansberry realized one day that it was finally finished. All she needed was a title. At first she tried "The Crystal Stair," a phrase from a poem by Langston Hughes, one of her favorite poets. In "Mother to Son," Hughes wrote, "Life for me ain't been no crystal stair, son."[6]

But flipping through the poet's other poems, Hansberry found exactly the right words in the poem "Harlem." "What happens to a dream deferred?" wrote Hughes. "Does it dry up, like a raisin in the sun?"[7] Excited by the image, Hansberry typed *A Raisin in the Sun* at the top of her first page.[8]

In the poem "Harlem" by Langston Hughes, Hansberry found the perfect title for her first play: *A Raisin in the Sun.*

The play seemed to do so many of the things she had planned, yet Hansberry knew she was no judge of how effective it was. That night, she read the script to Nemiroff. Dazzled by its power, he wondered about the next step. Neither of them knew anything about getting a play produced.[9]

Hansberry knew only that she yearned for others to hear her story, meet her characters, cry and cheer with them. But that meant presenting her play to an audience.

Her first impulse was to share the script with friends. She and Nemiroff invited Burt D'Lugoff and Phil Rose to dinner the following night. The guests gathered in the living room, almost as excited as their hosts. Both men knew how long Hansberry had worked on the play. But until this night, they had not heard any of it.

Hansberry began reading, first seated in an armchair, and then sprawled on the floor. Reading the whole play aloud took hours, but from the start she had everyone's attention. Then, late into the night, they all argued about the characters and action, asking her to reread whole scenes. D'Lugoff and Rose brought the characters to life with their comments. They talked about the Youngers as if they were real people. Hansberry answered their questions, knowing these friends liked her play. It wasn't just polite interest that kept them turning her ideas over and over.[10] When the guests finally left, she and Nemiroff fell into bed, exhilarated and exhausted.

At eight o'clock the next morning, they were awakened by the telephone. Phil Rose's call that morning turned Hansberry's world upside down. He made her an offer that she had never anticipated. Rose, who knew as little as Hansberry and Nemiroff about the professional theater of Broadway, wanted to produce *A Raisin in the Sun*!

7

LIKE A MOVING
TRAIN

Hansberry could hardly believe Phil Rose's words on the telephone that morning. It was so soon after hearing the play. The story she had clasped so closely to herself was about to be shared with a whole array of strangers.[1] In fact, she found it hard to imagine exactly what lay ahead. For the moment, all she knew was that Rose was on his way over with $500 and a contract.

Phil Rose did not know much more than Hansberry did about producing plays. An aspiring opera singer who had performed with regional companies, Rose was married to an actress. That was about the extent of his experience with the theater.[2]

But the night before, he had become a true believer in *A Raisin in the Sun*. His idea of producing the play was a little like Burt D'Lugoff and Bob Nemiroff's response when Rose needed a song to record: "Why not give it a try?"[3]

Writing a song, however, was a far cry from producing a play in the professional world of Broadway theater. For one thing, there was money to consider. Staging a play on Broadway was so expensive that costs had to be shared. Raising money for a play was like financing a business. Many individuals invested sums of money and shared in the profits.

As soon as Hansberry signed the contract, Rose swung into action. He approached Sidney Poitier to play the part of Walter Lee Younger. A handsome young actor, Poitier had appeared in several films but was not yet a star.

Poitier jumped at the chance to appear in the groundbreaking play. He knew that nothing like it had ever appeared on the New York stage. His part was a gift, an opportunity to play a recognizable human being in a serious drama about African Americans.[4] Knowing the play deserved a first-rate production, he recommended his former teacher and director, Lloyd Richards.

When Hansberry first met Richards, she knew at once that this gentle, soft-spoken man was the perfect director for her play. In his hands, she could expect a sensitive, thoughtful presentation. And she could see that Richards, like Poitier, respected both the play and the playwright.

In meetings that followed, the play became the center of a wheel, with Hansberry and Richards working on the script. They pored over each scene, each speech, and each character. Their purpose was to relate individual elements to the play's total structure. Hansberry rewrote and rearranged.

Phil Rose's next task took him along another spoke of the wheel, trying to raise $100,000, the estimated amount of money needed for a Broadway production in 1959. When a playwright was well known or the actors famous, raising money was relatively easy. A few investors would offer large sums, confident of making a profit. But *A Raisin in the Sun,* with its brand-new author and little-known cast, was in another category.

Rose scheduled readings for potential backers—people who had invested in other Broadway shows. But repeatedly, would-be investors turned him down. Almost to a person, they expressed their wariness about the play's subject. They could not believe that a serious play about African Americans would attract Broadway audiences.[5] No one had ever tried it before, and no one knew this young playwright. She didn't have a track record of hit plays to her credit. Nor was the director, Lloyd Richards, a familiar Broadway figure. Moreover, no big stars appeared in the cast.

Rose realized that he would have to approach less affluent people and expect smaller amounts of money from each one. In the end, after eighty readings, he had attracted 147 investors. At the time, it was the largest number of investors for a single play. Some investments were as little as $100; the largest was $750. For many, it was their first experience investing in a Broadway show. Each person who contributed represented a show of faith in a play that *had* to go on.[6]

As Lloyd Richards assembled the rest of the cast, Rose went on to his next task, booking a theater. The usual practice in the 1950s was to set an opening date in New York and start four weeks of rehearsals. Then the producer would take the cast and production out of town for tryouts. Cities like Wilmington, Delaware, and New Haven, Connecticut, as well as seven or eight other places, were tryout towns. In out-of-town previews, cast members perfected their acting, and set designers made sure that everything worked. Playwright and director added last-minute script changes. At the end of the previews, a play was polished and ready for its Broadway run.

A Raisin in the Sun departed from the usual route. Rose heard the doubts expressed by potential investors repeated in his conversations with Broadway theater owners. Over and over, people asked the same question: "Who could possibly want to see a play about a black family?"[7]

Theater owners were not interested in the play's artistic merit. "We just don't think this thing can run," they said.[8] Owners of Broadway theaters wanted long-running hits. Their worst nightmare was a play that closed soon after opening, leaving a theater empty for the rest of the season. Therefore, the theater owners looked for surefire hits. They were reluctant to take a chance on anything as unusual as Hansberry's play.

Another problem for Rose was a rule enforced by Equity, the actors' union. The union rule allowed lower rehearsal salaries for only four weeks. Beginning with the fifth week of rehearsals, full salaries were required. Naturally, to pay full salaries, the play had to open and earn money from ticket sales.

With the play ready for rehearsal and still no theater in sight, Rose took a chance. He gambled that out-of-town performances would generate favorable reviews, and that New York theater owners would then make him an offer. The gamble was enormous. If the play failed, the $100,000 investment would be lost!

Finding space for rehearsals was easier. Rose booked a small theater two flights up, over a Forty-second Street movie house. Rehearsals began with a lot of hope.

Richards had assembled an exciting cast. Hearing Claudia McNeil's experienced voice read the part of Mrs. Younger in audition, Lorraine knew this was the woman she had imagined. Ruby Dee was perfect as Ruth, Walter Lee Younger's wife. Many years later, Dee said that after reading the script, she had hoped for the part of Beneatha.[9] But once again, she was playing a supporting character. During script conferences, Dee listened quietly. When she spoke her lines, she was convincing as the wife who longed for a better life. Diana Sands was a dazzling Beneatha.

In rehearsals, Hansberry learned another side of Lloyd Richards. He radiated confidence in the actors and took pains to reassure them, even when he had suggestions to improve their performances. From time to time, Richards would rise from his seat out front and approach one of the actors. The action would stop while they had a whispered conversation. Then he'd signal for the scene to continue. Hansberry and Nemiroff never knew what he had said. But they noticed subtle changes in the acting.[10]

Going into rehearsals was like hopping aboard a moving train. The producer contracted for stage sets and costumes, consuming more investment money. While Rose struggled with business arrangements for the opening, he concealed the details from Hansberry, not wanting her to worry. She remained closeted with Richards, polishing the play.[11]

As the first out-of-town tryout in New Haven approached, Hansberry knew every scene by heart. She loved her play and wanted audiences to love it too. Most of all, she wanted her mother to be proud of it.[12]

Lloyd Richards (right) directs a rehearsal scene from *A Raisin in the Sun:* Sidney Poitier and Claudia McNeil kneel in the foreground as Ruby Dee (left) and Diana Sands observe in back.

At the first New Haven performance in January, Hansberry sat in the front at the Shubert Theater, with Nemiroff beside her. With no curtain, they stared into the stage set with the familiar South Side kitchen. The theater darkened, and Lloyd Richards stepped forward on the stage. The audience hushed as he began to introduce the first scene. Hansberry shivered violently.[13]

And then it was over—the first full performance of *A Raisin in the Sun* for a paying audience. The applause was deafening, and afterward the whole company laughed and cried together.

But Hansberry's most vivid moment came the next morning, when the hotel maid came to tidy her room. An Irish immigrant, the maid still spoke with the strong accent of her homeland. She told Hansberry that the play could have been about her own father and mother. Although the Youngers were an African-American family from the South Side of Chicago, the maid recognized the same kind of emotion and suffering that her own family had endured. Listening to her, Hansberry knew the play had succeeded in catching universal emotions. The fact that the woman was Irish, like Hansberry's favorite playwright, Sean O'Casey, was particularly thrilling.[14]

The company left New Haven relieved that the production worked. The set had not collapsed. No one came down with the flu. Luck was on their side.

Glowing reviews in New Haven papers should have overwhelmed the New York theater owners. But still no one offered Rose a theater. He took the play to Philadelphia for another week of previews. There the response was even more enthusiastic than in New Haven.

James Baldwin, whom Lorraine had met briefly at the Actors Studio reading of his play *Giovanni's Room*, later said:

> I had never in my life seen so many black people in the theater. And the reason was that never before, in the entire history of the American theater, had so much of the truth of black people's lives been seen on the stage. Black people ignored the theater because the theater had always ignored them.[15]

Like Hansberry, Baldwin knew that blacks recognized the characters in *A Raisin in the Sun*. Either they or people they knew had experienced the same problems as her characters. Baldwin came backstage to congratulate Hansberry, and together they left by a back door. A crowd surrounded her, and she borrowed Baldwin's pen to sign autographs while he held her handbag. Laughing, she said, "It only happens once." She was clearly enjoying the moment.[16]

The reviews in Philadelphia newspapers pierced the wall of resistance in New York. A representative of the Shubert theater chain told Rose, "Okay, we don't have a theater open at just this moment, but something is vacating, so we'll take the show to Chicago for a month. And then we'll bring it into New York."[17] Finally, the play had a home.

Although the Shubert organization was paying for the Chicago run and a New York theater would at last be available, Hansberry had mixed feelings about bringing the play to Chicago. Her brothers and sister now owned the family's real estate agency. They had continued their father's active work in housing integration. And they were paying a price for their efforts. In fact, the family was expecting the city to bring a civil action against the real estate agency. Concerned that the play would receive less than fair treatment in the press, Carl and Perry Hansberry urged the cancellation of the planned Chicago run.

But Phil Rose was undeterred. Despite the tension, the company headed for Chicago. Fortunately, Hansberry felt none of the hostility. All over the city she was celebrated as a local success. Everyone wanted to meet her and interview her and see the play. Along with the public fanfare, she enjoyed seeing family and friends. Best of all, Shauneille Perry, her cousin and best friend from childhood, was there. Now a writer and actress, Perry came to Chicago with her husband to add their cheers.

Extravagantly praised for its Chicago performances, the company returned to New York with high expectations for the real test—the first night on Broadway.

8

TALK OF THE TOWN

As the New York opening approached, the African-American community buzzed with anticipation. The popular culture was at last recognizing it in a serious way. On March 1, the American Society of African Culture in New York invited Hansberry to speak at its Black Writers Conference in Town Hall. In her speech, Hansberry urged black writers to plunge into the intellectual life of the nation.

Hansberry could hardly wait to see the title of her play on the theater marquee. As soon it was posted, she and Nemiroff rushed uptown to the Ethel Barrymore Theatre to take snapshots.[1]

Then there was the seemingly endless wait until opening night, March 11, 1959. Good press from the New Haven, Philadelphia, and Chicago previews had raised everyone's expectations. Still, New York was unique. New York theater critics were the most powerful in the nation. They had been credited with either making or breaking plays. The success of *A Raisin in the Sun* was riding on their words.

It would be hours or even days after opening night before the full impact of the critics' opinions would be felt. But from the first moments in the theater that night, Hansberry knew her play had touched the audience.[2] In *A Raisin in the Sun*, African Americans in particular recognized mothers, grandmothers, and young adults who could be seen every day in their neighborhoods.

Applause exploded at the end of the first act. During intermission, a cyclone of voices surrounded Hansberry. Shouts of praise topped questions and predictions.

In another part of the theater, Mamie Hansberry laughed when asked her opinion of the play. "She's my sister," Mamie replied. "So I may be biased!"[3]

Hansberry need not have worried about her mother's response to the play. One reviewer overheard Mrs. Hansberry's proud comment, "That's my daughter!"[4]

The supreme moment came after the final curtain fell. Sidney Poitier swept Hansberry onto the stage

Lorraine Hansberry was thrilled to see the title of her play
A Raisin in the Sun on the marquee of a Broadway theater.

where she looked down on the excited, cheering crowd. Later, at the cast party, telegrams began to arrive. One message in particular thrilled her. It came from prizewinning playwright Tennessee Williams, whose own new play, *Sweet Bird of Youth*, had just previewed in Philadelphia.[5]

Until the morning papers hit the newsstands with the first reviews, no one could totally relax. Anxious to file their columns before the papers went to press, the critics had been the first to leave the theater. With carefully guarded expressions, they gave no clue to their opinions.

Reviews from the most influential critics, Brooks Atkinson of *The New York Times* and Walter Kerr of *The New York Herald-Tribune*, arrived that night. Although both critics praised the play, their words seemed muted. Neither critic gave it a rave review. Hansberry balanced the mild reviews with the audience's overwhelming response. But Nemiroff wept at the critics' failure to recognize *A Raisin in the Sun* as a great play, important and groundbreaking. He wanted to read that a historic event had occurred that night at the Ethel Barrymore Theatre. Walter Kerr's words—that it was an "honest play," written by a talented young African-American woman—were simply not enough. Both Hansberry and Nemiroff went to bed that night feeling that the play had half failed.

The next morning raised their spirits. Reviews in

other papers made it absolutely clear that *A Raisin in the Sun* would be a huge success. By midday, worries about low ticket sales had vanished.[6]

More praise came in weekly and monthly magazines. A columnist for *The New Yorker* magazine wrote that "the cast is flawless and the teamwork on the first night was as effortless and exuberant as if the play had been running for 100 performances."[7]

Nemiroff found every review and became excited about each one. Hansberry praised him to one reporter, saying, "If it hadn't been for him, this play would never have hit the boards."[8]

Interviewers who came to the second-floor apartment on Bleecker Street were startled by Hansberry's youth. Barely twenty-nine years old, she looked even younger in casual brown corduroy pants and sneakers. Observing a reporter looking around the modest apartment, Hansberry said, "I'm a writer and this is a workshop. We're not celebrities or anything like that. But I am going to get the landlord to paint that hall."[9]

Newly famous, Hansberry was asked to write books, to adapt a mystery story for the movies, and to write musical versions of novels. She received many social invitations from people whom she had never met. Most of those she declined.

Requests to speak to African-American groups were harder to refuse. They were all doing such important work that, when approached in person or on the

One critic called the cast of *A Raisin in the Sun* "flawless." This scene shows Diana Sands (left), Claudia McNeil, and Edward Hall.

phone, she found herself accepting their invitations. But this kept her very busy, and she longed to get back to her writing. In just one day, she taped a television program, attended a tea, and made a quick change to go out to dinner with her husband. Then they were off to a reception honoring a young actor, Harold Scott, for whom Hansberry had promised to write a part in a future play.

In an interview for *The New Yorker*, Hansberry said, "I enjoy it actually, so much. I'm thrilled, and all of us associated with the play are thrilled. Meanwhile, it does keep you awfully *busy*. What sort of happens is you just hear from *everybody!*"[10]

But several newspaper and magazine articles raised issues that made Hansberry realize not everyone had completely understood the play. Reviewers sometimes referred to *A Raisin in the Sun* as an example of "naturalistic" writing. A type of play popular for the previous ten years or so, "naturalism" dealt with life as it was. Hansberry vehemently objected to the label. She had set out to write a "realistic" play, going beyond what her characters were, to show what they *could* be. For Hansberry, African-American potential was a crucial thread in her story.[11]

Then there were writers who claimed the play was not about African Americans at all, saying that her characters were no different from any working-class family. This idea, picked up and repeated in article after article, infuriated her. Like Sean O'Casey, her model, she had invented a specific family for her play. It was an African-American family living on the South Side of Chicago after World War II. "Not only is this a Negro family," Hansberry said, "but it's not even a New York family or a southern Negro family—it is specifically Southside Chicago. . . . to that extent they can become everybody. So I would say it is definitely a Negro play before it is anything else." Writers who repeated the fallacy did not understand. Hansberry was making a clear statement about the problems of African Americans living in the American culture.[12]

Another response in the same vein, that she was not really a black writer, troubled Hansberry. Recognizing the unwillingness to honor a successful nonwhite, she insisted that she was writing from her own experience as an African-American woman.[13] Hansberry's reaction to these misinterpretations revealed a feisty intellectual known to her former *Freedom* colleagues but not always visible in the happy, smiling woman seen in interviews.

The whirl of activity became a cyclone in April when the New York Drama Critics Circle voted *A Raisin in the Sun* the best dramatic play of the 1958–59 season. The phone began ringing off the hook once more as renewed publicity swept Hansberry into another round of interview and personal appearance requests.

Hansberry became the first African-American

woman and the youngest playwright honored by the New York drama critics, winning out over two famous writers. Tennessee Williams and Edward Albee, both of whom had written several excellent plays, were also in the running for the award. But their current plays lost to *A Raisin in the Sun*.

Not everyone agreed that the play merited such a prestigious award. At least one writer felt that Hansberry's youth and inexperience made the play's success a fluke, and that either Williams's or Albee's play deserved the award. Others maintained that the award was given to Hansberry because she was an African American working with what was then novel subject matter.

Hansberry took the criticism with good grace. In her heart she knew the strengths and weaknesses of her play, but she also realized that she was the target of racial bias. To one reviewer, she said, "If I received the award because I am a Negro, then that's the first award given to a Negro!"[14]

With all the fanfare, Hansberry did not get back to her writing until almost two months after opening night. She cherished having a day to herself and even looked forward to cleaning the apartment. She had always done the cleaning, believing that she, and no one else, should do it. As she told one interviewer, "I feel very strongly about that."[15]

Meanwhile more negative publicity began to surface.

Night after night, applause thundered through the Barrymore Theatre for the first serious Broadway drama about an African-American family.

The anticipated civil action against the Hansberry real estate agency in Chicago finally hit. Lorraine Vivian Hansberry was named in the lawsuit, although she had no active part in the agency. In fact, sometime earlier, family members had removed her name from the ownership papers.[16]

But the media took up the story of a "slum land-lord" turned playwright.[17] Hansberry refused to defend herself, believing that the issue had nothing to do with her as an artist. For her husband, the word "slum" was a particular irony. He vividly remembered the property named in the lawsuit. It was the graceful family home in which the Hansberrys had lived at the time of the Hansberry-Nemiroff marriage.

At least the slumlord stories slowed down her telephone calls. When playwright and friend James Baldwin telephoned one day, she told him with a laugh, "Jimmy, do you realize you're only the second person who's called me today? And you know how my phone kept ringing *before*?"[18]

With *A Raisin in the Sun* playing sold-out performances, plans for a movie developed. Hansberry wrote the screenplay, adapting the script for the screen and adding new scenes. Film made it possible to set the Youngers' apartment in the panorama of the South Side and the whole city of Chicago. But more important, Hansberry enriched her conception of the family's lives, with scenes that introduced tradespeople and employers. This expanded the film to more than three hours, but most of the additions landed on the cutting-room floor. Except for outdoor scenes, the final version essentially followed the play.

Honored with the Screenwriters Guild Award, the film also won a special award at the Cannes Film Festival in France. Although disappointed with the cuts, Hansberry expressed her overall satisfaction with the film.[19] Opening in 1961 with the play's original actors in the important roles, the film received enthusiastic reviews. The play had been performed for nineteen months on Broadway, but as a movie, Hansberry's story reached an even wider audience.

Hansberry bought a house a few blocks away in Greenwich Village with a larger apartment and soon discovered the woes of being a landlord. Remembering the cool, green countryside in Columbia, Tennessee, and the clear night skies at Camp Unity, she looked beyond the city for a sanctuary.

9

THE MOVEMENT

In the hills of Croton-on-Hudson, north of New York City, Hansberry and Nemiroff bought a house in August 1962. The trees and fields reminded Hansberry of her Grandmother Perry's home in Tennessee. She hung a sign, "Chitterling Heights," from a tree and went back to work.

Hansberry surrounded her work area with inspiring images. Photos of Paul Robeson and of Michelangelo's sculpture *David* looked down on her desk. She placed a bust of Albert Einstein nearby. A picture of her beloved O'Casey was in sight at the top of the stairs.

As usual, several projects claimed her attention.

The play about Africa, although still in rough draft, now had the title *Les Blancs*. And she had a name for the main character in her Greenwich Village script. She called him Sidney Brustein. At the same time, her fascination with Toussaint L'Overture, the Haitian rebel, was demanding its own play.

But in spite of the space and quiet of the country, she was having trouble making progress with any of the projects. Like many other creative people, Hansberry was experiencing something known as "writer's block." She recorded her difficulties in a journal. "I sit at this desk . . . and—nothing happens. I begin to think more and more of doing something else with my life while I am still young."[1]

Two weeks later, she was still struggling. "Have torn up another twenty pages . . . and now? What?"[2] Then, less than a week later, her mood changed. "Tonight," she wrote, "am in extraordinary spirits. Believe the last two years are truly behind me."[3]

Four days later, she made a breakthrough with the Sidney Brustein script. In her journal she exulted:

> The magic has come: about an hour ago! A torrent of what I have been trying to write all along. The people I know in the Village and not a stagey version of them. It will be all right now—a lot of work. But I know what I am writing now. It came all at once while I was in the kitchen and I wrote fourteen pages in an hour. . . . Thank God, thank God! I could not have stood much more.[4]

At their home near a small town north of New York City, Hansberry relaxes with her husband, Bob Nemiroff.

The year before, Hansberry had set aside a television script with the title *What Use Are Flowers?* After an unhappy experience with an earlier script, she had lost hope of having it produced.[5]

In 1960, producer-director Dore Schary had proposed a series of television dramas to commemorate the one-hundredth anniversary of the Civil War. The National Broadcasting Company announced that the series marked a return to serious television drama.

Commissioned to write the opening script in the series, Hansberry chose a realistic approach to slavery as her subject. She began research at the Main Reading Room of the New York Public Library, at the Schomburg Collection of Research in Black Culture in Harlem, and in her own books. In the *Congressional Record*, century-old newspapers, diaries of slaves, and other primary sources, she studied the historical context of her drama.

The play she wrote was nothing like *Gone With the Wind*, Margaret Mitchell's Civil War story that romanticized master-slave relations. Hansberry developed real characters and avoided demonizing the slave owner in her play. At the climax of the story, she departed from the conventional view of slavery. Master Hiram was a kind and benevolent slaveholder. Yet he could not control his own son, who blinded a young slave named Hannibal because the slave had learned to read. Hannibal's mother, Risa, rejected the notion that a master could control the lives of his slaves but not his own son. In the climax, Risa chose to save Hannibal and left the master to die.

Hansberry took her title, *The Drinking Gourd*, from a Negro spiritual sung by slaves escaping on the Underground Railroad. "Follow the drinking gourd" became a code for runaway slaves. It urged them to look to the skies and find the stars known as the Big Dipper for direction in their nighttime flights to freedom.

As Hansberry worked on her script, Dore Schary was encountering resistance at NBC television. Network executives were cool to the news that he had engaged Hansberry to write the first segment. When they asked about her point of view on the subject of slavery, he thought they were joking. "She's against it, of course," he said in a mock serious tone. No one laughed, and from that moment, Schary expected the worst.[6] But still hoping for support for the series, he kept the controversy from Hansberry. She finished the script, the only one ever completed in the series. After reading it, the popular film actor Henry Fonda agreed to play the lead role.

At no time did Schary suggest diluting the strong series he had imagined. He submitted to NBC what he later called Hansberry's "powerful, marvelous script," with outlines of the other segments.[7]

Hansberry read of the network's decision to cancel

Following the success of *A Raisin in the Sun*, Hansberry set out to write a script for a television drama called *The Drinking Gourd*.

the series in *The New York Herald-Tribune* on August 30, 1960. In a radio discussion at the start of the Civil War Centennial Year on January 1, 1961, she said, "They asked me for it . . . and then I read in the newspaper that some studio official . . . had attached a notation to it . . . 'superb' . . . *and then they put it away in a drawer. . . .* "[8]

Hansberry had originally conceived *What Use Are Flowers?*, a drama with vivid imagery, for film. However, the experience with *The Drinking Gourd* influenced her to adapt the second television script for the stage. Changing from television to a stage version required unique transitions, and she put it aside until she could finish two other plays-in-progress.

Hansberry knew that Americans were still not ready to confront the past. The Civil War had ended a century before, and the Supreme Court had ordered an end to school segregation in 1954. Yet there was still resistance to accepting African Americans as human beings entitled to equality.

Years before, when she left the staff of *Freedom*, Hansberry had decided to support the protests of African Americans with her writing. But now, with so many people risking their lives in the struggle for civil rights, she began to question herself. Should she take a more active role? she wondered.[9]

By the spring of 1963, no one in America could escape the ferocity of the civil rights conflict.

Nonviolent marches in Birmingham, Alabama, led by the Reverend Dr. Martin Luther King, Jr., had captured the headlines. In sixty-five days and nights of protest, thousands of southern civil rights workers were jailed. Determined to continue demonstrating, Dr. King recruited public school students for the marches.

The violent police reaction to the demonstrations burst upon TV screens in early May. High-pressure fire hoses swept civil rights marchers off their feet. Police dogs were filmed biting children as young as six years old. Two thousand more protesters were jailed after the resulting melee. Fearing race riots, President John F. Kennedy and Attorney General Robert Kennedy issued pleas for dialogue between the black and white communities.

Two weeks after a truce in Birmingham, Hansberry jumped into the fray. With other prominent African Americans, she confronted Attorney General Robert Kennedy at his New York apartment. Although Kennedy prided himself on his civil rights record, his visitors vehemently disagreed. In a marathon session, they accused him of insensitivity and failure to act decisively against the Birmingham police. One of the group, singer Lena Horne, suggested that Kennedy escort a southern black child to school as a concrete act of courage. That way, it would be clear that when someone spit on him, that person was spitting on the nation. The group was outraged when Kennedy rejected the idea as a meaningless gesture.

The visitors expected less talk and more action from the attorney general of the United States. After three hours of emotional accusations, Robert Kennedy felt baffled and angry. His visitors departed thinking that they had not reached him in any meaningful way.[10]

Hansberry and Nemiroff supported a group called the Student Non-Violent Coordinating Committee (SNCC, pronounced "snick"). Idealistic and determined, the students lacked organization and funds. With Burt D'Lugoff, Hansberry and Nemiroff sponsored fund-raising concerts and events at which they introduced the SNCC leaders. They persuaded nationally known folk singers Judy Collins and Bob Dylan to perform at fund-raisers.

One gathering in Croton raised money for a station wagon. Two northern students helping in the civil rights struggle drove the car to Mississippi in the summer of 1963. While organizing to increase voter registration among African Americans, those two students were murdered, along with their black co-worker. The names of Andrew Goodman, Michael Schwerner, and James Chaney became rallying cries for the end of racial segregation.

Hansberry's passion for justice erupted in public speeches, in television interviews, and in letters to editors. She denounced people who criticized the

African-American fight for equality. She made it clear that African Americans would play by the rules when the rules protected them. Hansberry minced no words in expressing her beliefs during interviews. She spoke as if she did not expect to be invited back.[11]

Television had brought the stark reality of racial discrimination and all its cruelty into America's homes. The Student Non-Violent Coordinating Committee captured the struggle in a book of photographs entitled *The Movement: Document of a Struggle for Equality*. The book included photos of significant events in fighting for equality. Boycotts, sit-ins at segregated lunch counters, lines of African Americans registering to vote for the first time, nonviolent marches, the Birmingham demonstrations—all were there. Hansberry agreed to write the text for this important book, fitting yet another project into her schedule. Her words matched the vivid images, honoring those who fought and died in the struggle for equal rights.

Juggling the book manuscript and the plays, Hansberry began to experience physical symptoms that were more than the fatigue and stress she could usually fight off. Something was seriously wrong.

10

TO BE YOUNG,
GIFTED, AND
BLACK

arly in April, not long before the confrontation with Attorney General Robert Kennedy, Hansberry had experienced what she referred to in her journal as a "weird attack." The doctor she consulted arranged for a hospital stay later in the month.[1]

Hansberry considered her physical condition a minor inconvenience and pushed on with her usual schedule. She even took several manuscripts from aspiring playwrights with her to the hospital. There she wrote critiques of the writers' work. Nemiroff typed one response, on which she scrawled an apology for its late arrival. Hospital tests seemed to indicate an ulcer, and Hansberry began a treatment program.

Never satisfied with the amount of writing she produced, Hansberry was impatient with herself. She had begun 1963 with two resolutions. First she renewed her commitment to write, and second, she resolved to train her German shepherd puppy, Chaka.[2]

Her favorite dramatic project, *Les Blancs*, was beginning to take shape. Steeped in African history, Hansberry brought a fresh understanding of Africa's future to the narrative. Long before African nations began to emerge from European rule, she had spoken of their coming independence.

In the 1950s, as a staff member of *Freedom*, she had advocated the end of colonial rule in Africa. Standing on street corners, she handed out petitions asking the government to free political prisoners. Exiles from South Africa and Rhodesia and exchange students from Kenya, Sierra Leone, and Nigeria had visited Hansberry and Nemiroff's apartment in the early years of their marriage. The young couple frequently joined the exiles on picket lines outside the United Nations and European consulates.

Hansberry's understanding of African history stemmed from study and wide reading. After arriving in New York, she attended a year-long seminar on Africa with W. E. B. Du Bois, the great African-American scholar. On her own, she soaked up the

Lorraine Hansberry learned a great deal about African-American history from the great African-American scholar and writer W. E. B. Du Bois.

works of every African and African-American historian she could find.

Since then, African nations, one by one, had shed their European rulers and formed new governments. In *Les Blancs*, Hansberry created a dramatic confrontation between the old, European-dominated Africa and the new. Her own experiences had taught her that European rulers in Africa, like American slaveholders, found it easy to justify exploiting blacks by asserting a false notion of white superiority. She believed that everyone shared the responsibility of challenging that notion.

Hansberry modeled her characters on Uncle Leo Hansberry's African students, whose careers she had followed. Several had become leaders in their countries. One of them, Nnamdi Azikewe, was the first president of the new nation of Nigeria. While Hansberry was working on *Les Blancs* in 1963, Nigeria named a school for Leo Hansberry—the new Hansberry College of African Studies in Lagos.

Playgoers first encountered Hansberry's interest in the new Africa in *A Raisin in the Sun*: Beneatha, the daughter, had a friend from college, Asagai, who was very much like African students Hansberry had known at the University of Wisconsin. When the play opened in 1959, Asagai seemed exotic to some theater critics. Others ignored him. But Hansberry had deliberately introduced him to show another side of Beneatha. She wanted Beneatha to represent educated African Americans of her own generation. Interested in history, they were passionate about forming a better world.

Two weeks before the opening of *A Raisin in the Sun,* Hansberry had addressed a group of African-American writers. In her speech she linked the destiny of African people with American blacks. Both groups shared a history of oppression. She urged the writers to participate in American and global intellectual affairs. In that way, they would become key players. Only the solidarity of all black people of the world, she believed, would free them from their bondage.

Hansberry struggled with *Les Blancs*. She knew the subject was complex. Without oversimplifying the issues, she wanted to clearly communicate her ideas to an audience. But she was not sure the play was working. She decided to take the finished Act One, Scene One to the writers' workshop at the Actors Studio for a reading.

Playwrights routinely arranged Actors Studio readings to promote discussions of their plays in progress. By listening to the audience's responses, writers learned what was strong in the plays and what parts still needed work. Hansberry had first met her friend James Baldwin at an Actors Studio writers' workshop during the reading of his play *Giovanni's Room*. Still inexperienced at that time, she lacked the confidence to present *A Raisin in the Sun* for a reading. Now, however, with a sureness born of her first success, she felt secure enough to ask for professional opinions. She engaged actors to play the parts in *Les Blancs* for an audience of other actors and writers.

After the scene, the audience sat stunned. As Hansberry had feared, even this sophisticated group of professional theater people failed to understand her story.[3] Something was wrong that only she could fix.

Knowing that *Les Blancs* required much more work, Hansberry put it aside and turned her attention to *The Sign in Sidney Brustein's Window*. For this play, Hansberry developed a character who was an idealist. At one time, Sidney Brustein had worked at making the world a better place. But time, a lack of success in solving problems, and events in his personal life had worn him down. Discouraged, he was tempted to stop trying. However, when challenged, Sidney once again took a stand for his principles.

In June, Hansberry spoke at a community gathering near her home in Croton. With her was Jerome Smith of the Congress of Racial Equality (CORE), who had also attended the meeting with Attorney General Robert Kennedy. CORE was another group organized to support civil rights activists in the South. Its workers were in the front lines of the struggle, and CORE had little use for pleas for patience, especially when they came from political leaders like the attorney general.

Smith's fiery challenge to Kennedy had set the tone of the earlier meeting.

As Hansberry introduced Smith to the Croton community, she expressed her pride in the young man. Her speech—entitled "We Are One People!"—reiterated her outrage at Kennedy's description of his prominent African-American visitors as "exceptional." Many members of the white community, including Kennedy, failed to recognize that on major matters of race, African Americans were united as one people. Both to Kennedy and at the Croton gathering, Hansberry stressed the solidarity that African Americans felt with one another, whether rich or poor. When one group of African Americans was attacked, all felt the sting. Regardless of their own advantages, professional and affluent blacks knew the suffering of their brothers and sisters in Birmingham, she said.[4]

Despite speeches, fund-raisers, and hospital stays, Hansberry's writing progressed. By New Year's Day, 1964, she felt confident enough about *The Sign in Sidney Brustein's Window* to look forward to its production. She could hardly wait to go back to work again on *Toussaint*. Even *Les Blancs*, which she had originally hoped to finish before *Sidney*, had improved with some revision.

Although few people knew it, Hansberry's marriage had been troubled for some time. She and Nemiroff quietly divorced in March 1964. Because of her illness, they agreed to tell only family and their closest friends about the breakup. But despite the divorce, they continued their professional relationship. Hansberry regularly consulted with Nemiroff about her plays-in-progress.

By April 1964, a full year after her first attack, Hansberry could no longer ignore the messages her body was sending. Not pain, but constant, disturbing discomfort left her sleepless despite sedatives. With little appetite, she rapidly lost weight. Then the pain returned, along with new symptoms.

Hansberry was diagnosed with pancreatic cancer, for which there was no cure. For the rest of the year, she was in and out of the hospital for surgery and cancer treatments. One day in May, she forced herself to leave the hospital for a speaking engagement with the United Negro College Fund. In her speech to the winners of a writing contest, she first used the phrase "young, gifted and black." She told the young writers that the world needed their gifts and stories.[5]

Although very ill, she also took part in an explosive Town Hall debate in June 1964. Billed as "The Black Revolution and the White Backlash," the panel included both whites and blacks. In the debate, Hansberry defended what people were calling the "extreme protests" of African Americans. She reminded the audience that the protests emerged from a long history of frustration. Her own commitment to the need for dialogue among all people was as firm as ever. She pointed out that white people had been among the first to die in the current civil rights struggle. Hansberry called on members of both races to take even greater risks to achieve civil rights for all.[6]

Late in July, Hansberry's doctor sent her to the Lahey Clinic in Boston for treatment. Returning to New York, she once again checked into University Hospital. With her, she carried drafts of the civil rights book, *The Movement,* and her almost completed play, *The Sign in Sidney Brustein's Window.*

Nemiroff continued to consult with her on *Sidney* and *Les Blancs.* Ready for rehearsals, *Sidney* met few of the financial problems that *A Raisin in the Sun* had encountered. Investors expected another successful play from the award-winning writer.

Hansberry moved into the Victoria Hotel to be close to rehearsals. She struggled to attend and take notes for revisions. To cast members, her eyes seemed enormous in a face thinned by pain and disease. On opening night, October 15, 1964, she barely made it to the Longacre Theatre. Seated in a wheelchair far back in the theater, she stayed for a short time to greet friends after the final curtain. Two days later, she called her old friend Burt D'Lugoff, who was also a doctor. He rushed her to the hospital. Lapsing into a coma, she was not expected to live another day. But after four days of unconsciousness, she rallied and gradually regained her strength. Although she knew she was seriously ill, she never lost hope of recovering and returning to her work.

The Sign in Sidney Brustein's Window was met with mixed reviews. Most of its characters were white, which puzzled critics. Why, they wondered, had the author of a stunning first play about her familiar African-American culture chosen a different direction?

The criticism surprised Hansberry. Her characters were based on intellectuals from many ethnic backgrounds whom she had known intimately in Greenwich Village. Sharing their idealism about working for a better world, she understood their motivation and behavior. Her play, she felt, presented believable people faced with choices and the temptation to do nothing. The main character's words and actions expressed Hansberry's own affirmation of life.

The lukewarm reviews immediately affected ticket sales. The play might have closed in a week or two but for the intervention of a whole array of Hansberry fans. True believers in the play's message, like Nemiroff and D'Lugoff, were determined to keep it going. However, they could not have succeeded by themselves. Theater people, clergy, and ordinary New Yorkers formed a committee to keep performances running on a week-to-week basis. They bought newspaper ads, arranged for radio announcements, and passed out flyers on Broadway. Actors called friends and urged them to see the play. Others spoke to groups that normally buy blocks of tickets for theater parties. Religious leaders who recognized the moral and spiritual questions addressed by the play talked about it in their churches and temples. The messages urged people to hurry to the theater to see the latest work by a prizewinning playwright.

In the months to come, traditionally the time of year when plays are least well attended, hundreds of people joined together to keep *Sidney* running. It was an incredible story of repeated closing notices that were canceled by a swelling of new support. Cast members took pay cuts. At one performance, the audience passed a hat for contributions. And every week, as if by a miracle, minimum ticket sales kept the play alive. It survived November and the slow weeks before Christmas. Then the show moved to Henry Miller's Theatre, where it revived a little during the holidays and crept into January.

For 101 performances, the play went on. In the hospital, Hansberry heard from Nemiroff and friends about the loving efforts that were keeping her play alive. Her sister, Mamie, stayed in New York during the last months. When she saw *Sidney*, Mamie was moved by a scene that came straight out of their childhood. Sidney's wife, Iris, talked about playing a game called the fish lady with her sister when she was little. As the fish lady, Iris cleaned the fish, which were her little sister's fingers. It was a game that Mamie had played with

The Sign in Sidney Brustein's Window received mixed reviews, but Hansberry's fans rallied their support to keep the show open.

Lorraine when she was little. Mamie realized how many things we tuck away into memory.[7]

The glorious rally ended on January 12, 1965, the day Hansberry died in University Hospital. Moments before she slipped into her last coma, she spoke the words of an old spiritual into her tape recorder. "My Lord calls me. He calls me by the thunder. I ain't got long to stay here."[8] The thunder of ideas that surrounded Lorraine Hansberry in life was stilled. At Henry Miller's Theatre, the lights went down on *The Sign in Sidney Brustein's Window* for the last time.

Hansberry's funeral, at the small Presbyterian Church of the Master in Harlem, drew more than six hundred mourners. Well-known entertainers sat beside beginning actors and playwrights. Faltering and sad at first, then gaining strength, the congregation sang an old hymn, "Abide with me, fast falls the eventide, the darkness deepens; Lord with me abide."

Dr. Martin Luther King, Jr., sent a sympathy message, which was read by the pastor, the Reverend Eugene Callender. Paul Robeson celebrated Hansberry in his rich, melodious voice. "Her roots," he said, "were deep in her people's history. As an artist she reflected the light and struggles of our day in her work."[9] He quoted from an African-American folk song that reminded him of his lost friend, "Sometimes I feel like an eagle in the air." In closing, Robeson said, "As Lorraine bids us farewell, she bids us keep our heads high and to hold on to our strength and powers, to soar like an eagle."[10]

Nemiroff had asked the actress Ruby Dee to speak at the funeral. Despite her shyness, she agreed. "She was an artist of real promise, beginning to shed light on the fear, pain and hope of our time," Dee told the crowd. The best description of her friend came from *The Sign in Sidney Brustein's Window*, Dee said, and she quoted from one of Sidney's speeches: "I care. I care about it all. It takes too much energy not to care. . . . The 'why' of why we are here is an intrigue for adolescents; the 'how' is what must concern the living."[11]

Hansberry was buried at Beth El Cemetery near her beloved Croton-on-Hudson. She had named Nemiroff her literary executor, and he sadly went about the task of organizing her papers.

Although Hansberry never felt she was producing enough, she had completed an amazing amount of work. In the years following her death, Nemiroff pulled together journals, letters, interviews, and drafts of poetry, prose, and drama to publish collections of her writing.

There were the two complete television scripts: *The Drinking Gourd*, written for NBC's Civil War Centennial drama series, and *What Use Are Flowers?*, the fantasy Hansberry had intended to adapt for the stage and then set aside. *Les Blancs*, four years in the writing, had presented dramatic problems that she resolved only at the end of her life. In discussions with Nemiroff, she outlined changes in the script. Pages from a semiauto-biographical novel, *All the Dark and Beautiful Warriors*, drafts of scenes for *Toussaint*, her opera about the Haitian revolutionary, and scenes deleted from the film version of *A Raisin in the Sun* were all filed away. Letters to newspapers, journal entries, random jottings of story ideas, and thoughts about the state of the world shared space with manuscripts. She lamented sadness in the world, and she celebrated heroics. In her journal, she documented struggles with plots and character. She celebrated, too, in those pages, breakthroughs in her writing when she achieved exactly what she had imagined.

Nemiroff read through all the papers, astounded by the volume and richness of thought. Even he, so close to her during the creative years, could hardly believe the extent of her writing.[12] Convinced that the work should be published, he pored over pages and notebooks. He searched for a way to present the different formats, some in mere fragments, to blend her ideas without losing their singular affirmations.

Nemiroff found the unifying theme among Hansberry's last public words in her May 1964 speech to the United Negro College Fund. There she had hailed winners of the fund's writing contest as "young, gifted, and black."

The words described Hansberry herself, who never

grew old. Two years after her death, radio station WBAI in New York commemorated the anniversary with a special broadcast. Nemiroff and a volunteer producer invited performers who had known and admired Hansberry to participate. For three months Nemiroff wrote, taped, and edited portions of published and unpublished work. A cast of sixty-one distinguished film and stage actors assembled to read Nemiroff's radio script. Among them was Hansberry's cousin Shauneille Perry.

The broadcast, in two parts, was seven and a half hours long. It included scenes from *A Raisin in the Sun* and *The Sign in Sidney Brustein's Window*, tapes of interviews with Hansberry, and panel discussions in which she had participated. Responses to the project, from professionals and the public, motivated Nemiroff to adapt the script for a stage production. A producer for a publicly funded theater planned to stage the play with the title *To Be Young, Gifted and Black*. When the project fell through, Nemiroff began adapting the material for publication in book form. Before he finished, another producer offered to stage the drama.

To Be Young, Gifted and Black opened at the Cherry Lane Theatre in January 1969. The theater was located in downtown New York City. At this small house, away from the glitz and high production costs of Broadway, the Cherry Lane production ran for twelve months. It was the longest run of the 1968–69

After Hansberry's death, Robert Nemiroff blended pieces of her unpublished writing with lines from her plays to create *To Be Young, Gifted and Black*, the longest-running play of the 1968–69 off-Broadway season.

off-Broadway season. The play inspired Hansberry's friend Nina Simone, the folk singer, to write a song with the same title. Simone's work became a popular piece, sung by many choruses.

When the play closed, it entered the repertory of works that say something meaningful to each new generation. A national company of actors toured the country with the drama, and in the years since, it has played on college campuses and in community theaters all over the country. Regional theaters have celebrated succeeding anniversaries of Hansberry's successes with productions of *To Be Young, Gifted and Black*. In 1972, the film version opened.

A year after the off-Broadway production, Nemiroff published his book adaptation with the same title. As with the play, the book followed the journey of a young artist in her own words. Its design made clear how Hansberry's philosophy of hope and love of human beings was forged in her early experiences. The realism that marked her dramatic work emerged from her own life as a young, African-American woman engaged in political struggle in the mid-twentieth century.

As literary executor, Nemiroff pored through Hansberry's files with the intent of publishing and producing more of her work. *Les Blancs*, the play she had labored over for four years and considered her best, was close to her vision when she died. In that last year of her life, while *Sidney* was approaching rehearsals, she continued to consult with Nemiroff over drafts of *Les Blancs*. Nemiroff worked with her early and revised scenes, integrating fragments and creating dialogue where necessary. Recalling their last conversations about her plans for the play, he tightened some lines and elaborated others. In creating a final draft, Nemiroff consulted with other professionals, some of whom had known and worked with Hansberry. Although Nemiroff credited those who contributed, he made clear that the play owed its original concept and much of its writing to Hansberry.

Les Blancs opened at the Longacre Theatre in New York on November 15, 1970. In the cast was Harold Scott, a young actor for whom Hansberry had promised in 1959 to write a role in a future play. When Nemiroff approached him to play the part, he told Scott this was the role she had written for him.[13]

Les Blancs, which confronted racial oppression head on, jolted the opening night audience. Few critics or playgoers caught the author's belief in humankind. Some believed that the play applauded revolution and murder. The play closed after a short run. Despite the negative response, Nemiroff published the play in book form two years later, in a volume that also included Hansberry's television scripts, *The Drinking Gourd* and *What Use Are Flowers?*

Nemiroff continued working with Hansberry's papers and promoting small productions of her plays.

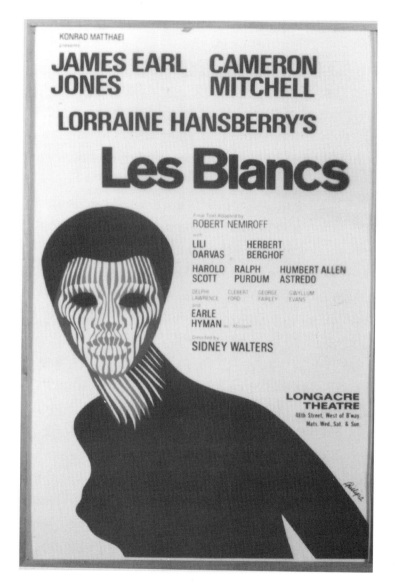

Hansberry worked on *Les Blancs* for four years before her untimely death. Robert Nemiroff then polished the play into its final version.

In the early 1970s, he collaborated with two young musicians on a musical version of *A Raisin in the Sun*. Captivated by the lyrical quality of the play, the musicians had composed a musical score during the last year of Hansberry's life. The musical adaptation, *Raisin*, produced by Nemiroff, opened on Broadway in 1974. Winner of the 1975 Tony Award for Best Musical of the Year, *Raisin* completed a long, successful New York run and then toured the country.

Translated into thirty languages, *A Raisin in the Sun* continues to draw audiences throughout the world. A breakthrough in dramatic art and subject matter, it prompted other expressions of the black experience. Theater professionals have recognized its place among America's great plays, some calling it a "classic."[14] Repeatedly, people return to the play and to Hansberry's later work, moved by her challenges and affirmations.

To celebrate the twenty-fifth anniversary of the New York opening of *A Raisin in the Sun*, Nemiroff prepared a new production, restoring cuts made in the original script. The restored version was performed in New York and at the Kennedy Center in Washington, D.C., in 1987. Two years later a new adaptation, with one additional scene, aired on public television. This American Playhouse production featured Danny Glover and Esther Rolle. It drew one of the largest viewing audiences in PBS history and was followed by a video release.

Esther Rolle and Danny Glover starred in the twenty-fifth-anniversary production of *A Raisin in the Sun*, which aired on PBS television. The groundbreaking play continues to draw audiences around the world.

Nemiroff prepared Hansberry's original screenplay of the film *A Raisin in the Sun* for book publication. This unfilmed screenplay was published in 1992, a year after Nemiroff's death.

Robert Nemiroff had devoted the last years of his life to ensuring that Hansberry's plays endured. In fulfilling his role as her literary executor, he succeeded in keeping her work alive. All over the nation, in middle schools, high schools, and colleges, students continue to study *A Raisin in the Sun* and *To Be Young, Gifted and Black*.

Hansberry's work has had an enormous impact on her own and succeeding generations. Her writing pulses with respect and wonder at the resilience of human beings. She saw beauty in the most downtrodden of lives and the possibility of redemption in the most hateful of people.

Lorraine Vivian Hansberry was only thirty-four years old when she died, a voice stilled too soon. No less than when she lived, her philosophy is needed today. Still needed is her cry against inhumanity, her advocacy of the powerless, and her call for people to work together and ensure justice for all. Lorraine Hansberry lived a short but full life, always true to her own vision of courage, civility, and compassion.

CHRONOLOGY

1930—Lorraine Vivian Hansberry is born on May 19 in Chicago, Illinois.

1938—The Hansberry family occupies a house in a white area to challenge housing discrimination practices; when the city orders them to move out, Lorraine's father, Carl Hansberry, files a lawsuit.

1940—The Supreme Court rules on Carl Hansberry's case that the housing discrimination practices are illegal.

1945—Carl Hansberry dies.

1948—Graduates from Englewood High School and enrolls at the University of Wisconsin.

1950—Moves to New York City, joins the staff of
–1952 *Freedom*, an African-American newspaper, engages in civil protests; enrolls at the New School.

1952—Becomes associate editor of *Freedom*.

1953—Marries Robert Nemiroff, a graduate student at New York University; resigns from *Freedom* but continues to write occasionally for the paper.

1956—Nemiroff and friend Burt D'Lugoff write hit song "Cindy, Oh Cindy"; the song's success makes full-time writing possible for Hansberry.

1957—Completes her play *A Raisin in the Sun*.

1959—*A Raisin in the Sun* opens at the Ethel Barrymore Theatre and is awarded Best Play of the Year by the New York Drama Critics Circle. Hansberry becomes the youngest American and the first African American to win the award.

1960—Writes *A Raisin in the Sun* screenplay and a never-produced television play, *The Drinking Gourd*; continues work on two plays, *Les Blancs* and *The Sign in Sidney Brustein's Window*, and an opera about the Haitian rebel Toussaint L'Overture.

1961—The Screenwriters Guild and the Cannes Film Festival honor *A Raisin in the Sun*.

1963—Undergoes two operations for cancer; supports the civil rights movement with fund-raisers, and writes text for a book of photographs: *The Movement: Documentary of a Struggle for Equality*.

1964—Hansberry and Nemiroff quietly divorce but continue their professional collaboration; *The Sign in Sidney Brustein's Window* opens to mixed reviews and Hansberry returns to the hospital two days later.

1965—Lorraine Hansberry, age thirty-four, dies on January 12; *The Sign in Sidney Brustein's Window* closes that night.

1969—Nemiroff publishes a collection of Hansberry's
–1991 writing, *To Be Young, Gifted and Black*, in both play and book form; the play *Les Blancs*; and two television scripts, *The Drinking Gourd* and *What Use Are Flowers?* He produces a twenty-fifth anniversary production of *A Raisin in the Sun* for theater, public television, and video; his production *Raisin*, based on Hansberry's original play, wins the 1975 Tony Award for Best Musical.

CHAPTER NOTES

Chapter 1. Opening Night

1. Mamie Hansberry Mitchell, telephone interview with the author, July 13, 1976, transcript, p. 6.

2. Lorraine Hansberry, *To Be Young, Gifted and Black: Lorraine Hansberry in Her Own Words*, adapted by Robert Nemiroff (Englewood, N.J.: Prentice Hall, 1969), p. 91.

3. Ibid.

4. Margaret B. Wilkerson, "Lorraine Vivian Hansberry," *Black Women in America, An Historical Encyclopedia* (New York: Carlson, 1993), pp. 524–525.

5. Hansberry, p. 138.

6. Lorraine Hansberry, "The Beauty of Things Black—Toward Total Liberation: An Interview with Mike Wallace," May 8, 1959, recorded on *Lorraine Hansberry Speaks Out: Art and the Black Revolution* (Caedmon Records, 1972).

7. E. B. White, "Talk of the Town," *The New Yorker*, May 9, 1959, p. 33.

8. Ibid.

9. Ibid., p. 34.

Chapter 2. On the South Side of Chicago

1. Lorraine Hansberry, *To Be Young, Gifted and Black: Lorraine Hansberry in Her Own Words*, adapted by Robert Nemiroff (Englewood, N.J.: Prentice Hall, 1969), p. 36.

2. Ibid., p. 37.

3. Mamie Hansberry Mitchell, telephone interview with the author, July 13, 1976, transcript, p. 3.

4. Ibid.

5. Robert Nemiroff, personal interview with the author, August 1, 1976, transcript, p. 26.

6. Ibid.

Chapter 3. Other Voices

1. Lorraine Hansberry, *To Be Young, Gifted and Black: Lorraine Hansberry in Her Own Words*, adapted by Robert Nemiroff (Englewood, N.J.: Prentice Hall, 1969), p. 39.

2. Ibid., p. 25.

3. Shauneille Perry Ryder, telephone interview with the author, July 10, 1976, transcript, p. 2.

4. Mamie Hansberry Mitchell, telephone interview with the author, July 13, 1976, transcript, p. 4.

5. Ibid., p. 5.

6. Ibid., p. 1.

7. Shauneille Perry Ryder, letter to the author, August 9, 1976, p. 2.

8. Mitchell interview, p. 4.

9. Robert Nemiroff, personal interview with the author, August 1, 1976, transcript, p. 21.

Chapter 4. The First Melody

1. Mamie Hansberry Mitchell, telephone interview with the author, July 13, 1976, transcript, p. 2.

2. Robert Nemiroff, personal interview with the author, August 1, 1976, transcript, p. 23.

3. Lorraine Hansberry, *To Be Young, Gifted and Black: Lorraine Hansberry in Her Own Words*, adapted by Robert Nemiroff (Englewood, N.J.: Prentice Hall, 1969), p. 49.

4. Ibid., p. 50.

5. Margaret B. Wilkerson, "Lorraine Vivian Hansberry," *Black Women in America, An Historical Encyclopedia* (New York: Carlson, 1993), p. 524.

6. Hansberry, p. 65.

7. Ibid.

8. Nemiroff interview, p. 21.

9. Mitchell interview, p. 2.

10. Ibid.

Chapter 5. Harlem Street Corners

1. Mamie Hansberry Mitchell, telephone interview with the author, July 13, 1976, transcript, p. 2.

2. Lorraine Hansberry, "Negroes Cast in Same Old Roles in TV Shows," *Freedom*, June 1951, p. 7.

3. Lorraine Hansberry, *To Be Young, Gifted and Black: Lorraine Hansberry in Her Own Words*, adapted by Robert Nemiroff (Englewood, N.J.: Prentice Hall, 1969), p. 88.

4. Ibid., p. 78.

5. Ibid., p. 77.

6. Lorraine Hansberry and Stan Steiner, "Cry for Colonial Freedom Jolts Phony Youth Meeting," *Freedom*, September 1951, p. 3.

7. Lorraine Hansberry, "Women Voice Demands in Capital Sojourn," *Freedom*, October 1951, p. 6.

8. Hansberry, *To Be Young, Gifted and Black*, p. 79.

9. Robert Nemiroff, personal interview with the author, August 1, 1976, transcript, p. 39.

10. Hansberry, *To Be Young, Gifted and Black*, p. 87.

11. Ibid., p. 89.

12. Ibid., pp. 87–88.

13. Nemiroff interview, p. 18.

Chapter 6. A Small White Desk

1. Lorraine Hansberry, *To Be Young, Gifted and Black: Lorraine Hansberry in Her Own Words*, adapted by Robert Nemiroff (Englewood, N.J.: Prentice Hall, 1969), p. 89.

2. Mamie Hansberry Mitchell, telephone interview with the author, July 13, 1976, transcript, p. 3.

3. Robert Nemiroff, personal interview with the author, August 1, 1976, transcript, p. 4.

4. Lorraine Hansberry, "We Have So Much to Say," interview with Ted Poston, *The New York Post*, March 22, 1959, p. 2.

5. Lorraine Hansberry, "Make New Sounds: Studs Terkel

Interviews Lorraine Hansberry, May 22, 1959," *American Theatre*, November 1984, pp. 5–8.

6. Langston Hughes, *Collected Poems* (New York: Knopf, 1951), p. 30.

7. Ibid., p. 426.

8. Nemiroff interview, p. 12.

9. Ibid., p. 9.

10. Hansberry/Poston interview, March 22, 1959, p. 2.

Chapter 7. Like a Moving Train

1. Robert Nemiroff, personal interview with the author, August 1, 1976, transcript, p. 9.

2. Ibid., p. 7.

3. Ibid., p. 9.

4. "Negro Talent in a Prize Play," *Life*, April 17, 1959, pp. 142, 143.

5. Nemiroff interview, p. 32.

6. Sam Zolotow, "*A Raisin in the Sun* Basks in Praise," *The New York Times*, March 13, 1959, p. 25.

7. Nemiroff interview, p. 32.

8. Ibid., p. 33.

9. Ruby Dee, comments at "Lorraine Hansberry: Crossing Over Her Bridge, A Joint Celebration of Her Life and Work," symposium on Lorraine Hansberry, commemorating the thirtieth anniversary of her death, New Brunswick, N.J, April 8, 1995.

10. Nemiroff interview, p. 10.

11. Ibid.

12. Lorraine Hansberry, *To Be Young, Gifted and Black: Lorraine Hansberry in Her Own Words*, adapted by Robert Nemiroff (Englewood, N.J.: Prentice Hall, 1969), p. 91.

13. Nemiroff interview, p. 30.

14. Ibid., p. 38.

15. James Baldwin, "Sweet Lorraine," in *The Price of the*

Ticket, Collected Nonfiction 1948–1985 (New York: St. Mark's/Marek, 1985), p. 444.

16. Ibid.

17. Nemiroff interview, p. 34.

Chapter 8. Talk of the Town

1. Robert Nemiroff, personal interview with the author, August 1, 1976, transcript, p. 36.

2. Ibid., p. 35.

3. Mamie Hansberry Mitchell, telephone interview with the author, July 13, 1976, transcript, p. 6.

4. "People Are Talking About," *Vogue*, June 1959, p. 78.

5. Nemiroff interview, p. 37.

6. Ibid.

7. Kenneth Tynan, "Critics' Round Table," review of *A Raisin in the Sun, The New Yorker*, March 21, 1959, p. 101.

8. Lorraine Hansberry, "We Have So Much to Say," interview with Ted Poston, *The New York Post*, March 22, 1959, p. 2.

9. Ibid.

10. E. B. White, "Talk of the Town," *The New Yorker*, May 9, 1959, p. 33.

11. Lorraine Hansberry, "Make New Sounds: Studs Terkel Interviews Lorraine Hansberry," *American Theatre*, November 1984, p. 7.

12. Ibid.

13. Nemiroff interview, p. 38.

14. Lorraine Hansberry, "The Beauty of Things Black— Toward Total Liberation: An Interview with Mike Wallace," May 8, 1959, recorded on *Lorraine Hansberry Speaks Out: Art and the Black Revolution* (Caedmon Records, 1972.

15. White, p. 33.

16. Nemiroff interview, pp. 2, 3.

17. Ibid., p. 3.

18. James Baldwin, "Sweet Lorraine," in *The Price of the*

Ticket, Collected Nonfiction 1948–1985 (New York: St. Mark's/Marek, 1985), p. 445.

19. Lorraine Hansberry, *A Raisin in the Sun . . . The Unfilmed Original Screenplay*, Robert Nemiroff, ed. (New York: Plume, 1992), p. xxix.

Chapter 9. The Movement

1. Lorraine Hansberry, *To Be Young, Gifted and Black: Lorraine Hansberry in Her Own Words*, adapted by Robert Nemiroff (Englewood, N.J.: Prentice Hall, 1969), p. 169.

2. Ibid., p. 171.

3. Ibid., p. 178.

4. Ibid., p. 186.

5. Robert Nemiroff, "A Critical Background for *What Use Are Flowers?*" in Lorraine Hansberry, *Les Blancs: The Collected Last Plays of Lorraine Hansberry*, Robert Nemiroff, ed. (New York: Random House, 1972), p. 318.

6. Robert Nemiroff, "A Critical Background for *The Drinking Gourd*," in Hansberry, Les Blancs, p. 194.

7. Ibid., p. 199.

8. Ibid., p. 191.

9. Hansberry, *To Be Young, Gifted and Black*, p. 249.

10. John Donahue, "Bench Marks," *America*, January 20, 1979, p. 30.

11. Julian Mayfield, "Lorraine Hansberry: A Woman for All Seasons," *Freedomways*, 1979, p. 265.

Chapter 10. To Be Young, Gifted, and Black

1. Lorraine Hansberry, *To Be Young, Gifted and Black: Lorraine Hansberry in Her Own Words*, adapted by Robert Nemiroff (Englewood, N.J.: Prentice Hall, 1969), p. 218.

2. Ibid., p. 217.

3. Robert Nemiroff, "A Critical Background for *Les Blancs*," in Lorraine Hansberry, *Les Blancs: The Collected Plays of Lorraine Hansberry*, Robert Nemiroff, ed. (New York: Random House, 1972), p. 44.

4. Hansberry, *To Be Young, Gifted and Black*, p. 220.

5. Ibid., pp. 256–257.

6. Ibid., pp. 238–239.

7. Mamie Hansberry Mitchell, telephone interview with the author, July 13, 1976, transcript, p. 6.

8. James Baldwin, "Lorraine Hansberry at the Summit," *Freedomways*, 1979, p. 272.

9. William F. Farrell, "Six Hundred Attend Hansberry Rites; Paul Robeson Delivers Eulogy," *The New York Times*, January 17, 1965, p. 88.

10. Ibid.

11. Ibid.

12. Robert Nemiroff, foreword to Lorraine Hansberry, *To Be Young, Gifted and Black*, pp. xiii–xviii.

13. Harold Scott, comments at "Lorraine Hansberry: Crossing Over Her Bridge, A Joint Celebration of Her Life and Work," symposium on Lorraine Hansberry, commemorating the thirtieth anniversary of her death, New Brunswick, N.J., April 8, 1995.

14. Jewell Gresham Nemiroff, foreword to Lorraine Hansberry, *A Raisin in the Sun, The Unfilmed Original Screenplay*, Robert Nemiroff, ed. (New York: Plume, 1992), p. xix.

FURTHER READING

Bond, Jean Carey, and Esther Jackson. "Lorraine Hansberry: Art of Thunder, Vision of Light." *Freedomways*, no. 194, 1979.

Carter, Steven R. *Hansberry's Drama: Commitment Amid Complexity*. Chicago: University of Chicago Press, 1991.

Hansberry, Lorraine. *Les Blancs: The Collected Last Plays of Lorraine Hansberry*. Edited, with critical backgrounds, by Robert Nemiroff. New York: Random House, 1972.

———. *A Raisin in the Sun*. New York: Random House, 1959.

———. *A Raisin in the Sun . . . The Unfilmed Original Screenplay*. Edited by Robert Nemiroff. New York: Plume, 1992.

———. *The Sign in Sidney Brustein's Window*. New York: Random House, 1965.

———. *The Movement: Documentary of a Struggle for Equality*. New York: Simon & Schuster, 1964.

———. *To Be Young, Gifted and Black: Lorraine Hansberry in Her Own Words*. Adapted by Robert Nemiroff. Englewood, N.J.: Prentice Hall, 1969.

McKissack, Patricia, and Fredrick L. McKissack. *Young, Black, and Determined: A Biography of Lorraine Hansberry*. New York: Holiday House, 1997.

Tripp, Janet. *Lorraine Hansberry*. San Diego, Calif.:, Lucent, 1997.

Audiovisual Sources

Lorraine Hansberry: *The Black Experience in the Creation of Drama*. Princeton, N.J.: Films for the Humanities, 1976.

Lorraine Hansberry Speaks Out: Art and the Black Revolution. Selected and edited by Robert Nemiroff. New York: Caedmon Records, 1972.

A Raisin in the Sun. Los Angeles: Videotape production by Fireside Entertainment Company and KCET, 1998.

On the Internet

<http://www.scils.rutgers.edu/~cybers/hansberry.html>

INDEX